Cambridge Elements

Elements in Shakespeare and Text
edited by
Claire M. L. Bourne
The Pennsylvania State University
Rory Loughnane
University of Kent

EDITING AN EARLY MODERN PLAY

A Practical Guide

Suzanne Gossett
Loyola University Chicago

Gordon McMullan
King's College London

Shaftesbury Road, Cambridge CB2 8EA, United Kingdom

One Liberty Plaza, 20th Floor, New York, NY 10006, USA

477 Williamstown Road, Port Melbourne, VIC 3207, Australia

314–321, 3rd Floor, Plot 3, Splendor Forum, Jasola District Centre,
New Delhi – 110025, India

Cambridge University Press is part of Cambridge University Press & Assessment,
a department of the University of Cambridge.

We share the University's mission to contribute to society through the pursuit of
education, learning and research at the highest international levels of excellence.

www.cambridge.org
Information on this title: www.cambridge.org/9781009405584

DOI: 10.1017/9781009405607

© Suzanne Gossett and Gordon McMullan 2026

This publication is in copyright. Subject to statutory exception and to the provisions
of relevant collective licensing agreements, no reproduction of any part may take
place without the written permission of Cambridge University Press & Assessment.

When citing this work, please include a reference to the DOI 10.1017/9781009405607

First published 2026

A catalogue record for this publication is available from the British Library

A Cataloging-in-Publication data record for this Element is available from the Library of Congress

ISBN 978-1-009-40558-4 Paperback
ISSN 2754-4257 (online)
ISSN 2754-4249 (print)

Cambridge University Press & Assessment has no responsibility for the persistence
or accuracy of URLs for external or third-party internet websites referred to in this
publication and does not guarantee that any content on such websites is, or will remain,
accurate or appropriate.

For EU product safety concerns, contact us at Calle de José Abascal, 56, 1°, 28003
Madrid, Spain, or email eugpsr@cambridge.org

Editing an Early Modern Play

A Practical Guide

Elements in Shakespeare and Text
DOI: 10.1017/9781009405607
First published online: March 2026

Suzanne Gossett
Loyola University Chicago

Gordon McMullan
King's College London

ABSTRACT: More than half a century ago Clifford Leech published a useful essay called 'On editing one's first play', intended to 'save newly commissioned editors from a sense of frustration and an expense of time' by providing 'some guiding-lines'. The intervening years have seen massive changes in attitudes towards editing and in the technical expertise required. Neither editor nor reader can any longer be assumed to be white, male and Christian, or trained in the classics and the Bible. Editing is now recognized as a crucial intersection between critical and textual theory. Yet the skills required are not usually taught in graduate schools, and many competent scholars are uncomfortable answering such questions as 'what do editors actually do when they edit an early modern play?' This Element focuses both on the practical steps of editing (e.g., choosing a base text, modernizing, emending, etc.) and the theoretical premises underlying editorial decisions.

KEYWORDS: text, editing, modernization, emendation, commentary

© Suzanne Gossett and Gordon McMullan 2026

ISBNs: 9781009405584 (PB), 9781009405607 (OC)
ISSNs: 2754-4257 (online), 2754-4249 (print)

Contents

1. Preface, or, How to Cook an Edition — 1
2. Practice — 9
3. Theory — 75

1 Preface, or, How to Cook an Edition

This Element falls into three sections: this preface, a lengthy section on practice, and a much briefer section on theory. The latter two appear to be in the wrong order, we know, but we will explain this in due course. In this preface, we write in a fairly personal way. After that, we will attempt to write more objectively, but it is important to realize that there is a great deal in the business of editing that can never be objective – and anyway we both have opinions, and they aren't always shared opinions. If the writers of this little book – long-standing friends and collaborators in more than one series of early modern play editions – don't agree about certain things, then imagine how many differing opinions there are in the world of editing. This constant struggle can be tiring – arguments about apparently minor textual matters can be ferocious, and debates about authorship, in particular, tend too often to descend to personalities – but it can also be exhilarating because it underlines the second most important thing you need to know about editing, which is what we were both told by the editorial mentor we share, Richard Proudfoot. 'This is *your* edition', he would say when, in the wake of discussion, a decision had to be made: 'If you can argue your case, I will be happy to accept it'. In other words, your general editor, assuming you have one, may often be right and you wrong – and she will let you know when this is the case – but in the end the edition, and the choices made in that edition, are yours.[1] This is, we believe, one of the truly wonderful things about editing: editions of early modern plays may seem uniform in their structure and appearance, but all editions worth their salt are those of editors doing their own thing and doing it well.

That your edition is *your* edition is the second most important thing you need to know when you begin to edit. What, then, is the first most important thing? (Other, that is, than the most obvious requirement of any edition: that

---

[1] We should note that we have written this Element primarily with professional colleagues in mind – those of our peers who have not yet edited but may wish to do so. But it may well be that you are reading this as a student undertaking an editing task. If so, welcome to the joys of editing! For 'general editor', please read 'instructor' throughout.

it be accurate and defensible.) The answer is best embodied in another question: 'Who are your readers?' Because editing is only ever done for readers, and your decisions, including basic questions such as whether you are going to modernize early modern spelling and punctuation, must always be made in relation to your expected readership. It is worth stating clearly here and now: editions are for readers (and sometimes for those who will move from reading to staging), which means that each decision you make is made for those who will *use* your edition.

We have written this Element primarily for people editing for the first time or thinking about the possibility of editing; we hope it will also have value for people who are interested in understanding more about the processes of editing or are simply curious to know what editors *do* when they edit a play for a series such as Arden, Revels or Cambridge or as part of a collected works such as the *Norton Shakespeare*. An Element, with its signature 30 K word count, is not, cannot be, a comprehensive guide to editing, never mind to textual studies more broadly. As we proceed, we make suggestions for further reading, and we urge you to immerse yourself in the foundational bibliographical work of scholars such as W. W. Greg, R. B. McKerrow and A. W. Pollard, as well as in the most recent textual scholarship. If you are editing for a series, your general editors will provide you with thorough, canon-specific editorial guidelines; you may also wish to consult substantive online resources such as the 'Guidelines for Editors of Scholarly Editions' provided by the Modern Language Association of America (MLA).

Our aim in this Element is, by contrast, to offer a toehold for the new editor by demystifying the editing process. We are, we should note right away, by no means the first to do this. Much of what we do here serves to update Clifford Leech's invaluable 'On Editing One's First Play', published half a century ago – a sane, humorous, deeply informed and generous essay but one now unavoidably dated (not only in its references to card indexes and 'cyclostyling' but also in its habit of using the masculine pronoun for editors and general editors).[2] We believe an updating of Leech's essay has

---

[2] Clifford Leech, 'On Editing One's First Play', *Studies in Bibliography* 23 (1970), 61–70.

value, notwithstanding the extent to which textual matters have become part of mainstream Shakespeare criticism over the last few decades. Many scholars of Shakespeare and early modern drama, including some of the most highly regarded, still tend not to know anything, or anything much, about the business of editing, and some may still have a residual sense that editing is a secondary kind of intellectual activity. For both of us during our graduate years there was complete consistency on this issue. Smart people, we were given to understand, wrote critical monographs; people who weren't smart enough to write monographs edited. It never occurred to GM that he would edit a play until he was asked to edit *Henry VIII* for the Arden Third Series; editing was not something he had considered for his doctoral work.[3] SG, similarly, did not know she wanted to edit until she found a group of unknown, unedited early seventeenth-century dramatic manuscripts in the English College in Rome and then had to teach herself appropriate methods of editing them.[4]

Attitudes, happily, have changed. This is in part a result of the emergence of a field of study known as 'the sociology of the text', which at a crucial moment in the 1990s created a bridge between critical and textual theory, drawing impetus from certain aspects of poststructuralism for a rethinking of textual theory. We will say more about the 'sociology of the text' in Section 3, but the point is that the field of textual editing is now substantially occupied by people who straddle the critical/textual gulf, who both write critical monographs and edit texts and do not see a yawning divide either between these academic genres or between the roles of textual editor and literary critic and for whom the overlaps are far more important than the differences. Moreover, a generation of critically trained scholars who engaged with textual matters during their graduate years, especially in the United States, is now at associate or full professor level and has found ways to make the issues that arise from textual studies fascinating for their

---

[3] Gordon McMullan, ed., *Henry VIII*, The Arden Shakespeare, Third Series (Bloomsbury Publishing, 2000).

[4] Anon., *Blame Not Our Author*, ed. Suzanne Gossett (Malone Society Collections XII, 1983); Anon., *Hierarchomachia or The Anti-Bishop*, ed. Suzanne Gossett (Bucknell University Press, 1982).

students. The attention to text required for editing even a short passage from an early modern play has, we have found, a significant pedagogical payoff in leading students to close and closer reading.

Who, then, might wish to edit an early modern play? Please keep reading if you:

- Love early modern drama in all its gnarly, uplifting, bewildering gloriousness and all its bounding energy, across all its genres, and for its ability to transport you four centuries back to a truly extraordinary period of culturally and politically engaged theatrical creativity.
- Love the text. All of the text, we mean – the subplots as well as the main plots, the sections by the writer nobody cares about as well as those by that writer's famous collaborator, the central elements as well as the apparently subordinate elements such as paratext.
- Love the sound, the words, the rhythm, the fine twisty recalcitrant details of the text.
- Love pursuing the meanings of aspects of the text that are not transparent to twenty-first-century readers and refuse to rest until those meanings begin to emerge.
- Wish to offer your readers – especially students coming to the play for the first time – a reading experience that will be both pleasurable and informative.
- Are genuinely interested in acquiring a new and generative intellectual skill set.
- Are temperamentally uninclined to cut corners yet happy to work to a fairly rigorous timetable.
- Can keep your ego at bay when working out what your reader needs. Humility is essential. Editing is service; editing is pedagogy.
- Are simply curious to find out about editing or about aspects of textual studies with which you have not previously engaged.

The unavoidable thing about editing a play – the real challenge and joy – is that you have no choice but to tackle *every* element with equal gusto or your edition will be lacking. We have seen people fall at various fences when trying to edit, and it is usually either because they came simply to realize that editing does not suit them (a good and honest reason) or because they want to cut corners or skip some of the hard bits (not such a good reason). You may not know if editing will suit you until you try it. You may well surprise yourself by loving it. But if you try editing and find it doesn't suit you, then probably you should leave it alone – though we do think that developing the skills needed by an editor will make you a better critic, whether or not you ever actually edit.

But as long as you care about texts and their origins and their quirks and about both the minutiae and the big picture, then editing is for you. And by 'you' we do not only mean a White Anglo-Saxon male from the United States or the United Kingdom. Such persons are very welcome to be editors (half of this Element's writing team is one), but so is everybody else. The field of editing has long been preponderantly male, and that this has visibly become far less the case in the first quarter of the twenty-first century is a hugely welcome development. Still, while the days are long gone when editors were nearly all men, patriarchy has not disappeared, the skillset of editing was created almost exclusively by men, and work must still be done to ensure that gender balance is sustained. Moreover, gender equality is only one form of equality, and the greater the diversity of editors, the greater the intellectual and cultural diversity there will be within the ostensibly uniform frame of the critical edition. For scholars of colour, for global-majority scholars, the field will almost certainly look exclusively both white and US/UK/Canada-based – something that is changing, happily, as a new generation of general editors chooses its teams. We have written this Element in the hope that it will contribute to this crucial and necessary development.

Editing is a leveller. One of the mildly disconcerting things about agreeing to edit your first play is that no matter how experienced a critic you are, you are about to become a beginner again. This can be challenging. The best editors often have healthy egos (we will not name names), but they are also people who know what they don't know and deal pretty ruthlessly with the gaps in their knowledge. You are, after all, going to do this properly, or what's the point of starting? You will begin by learning the conventional language of editing – which we outline lightly in this Element – and you may well need to become familiar with an encoding language if you are, as is increasingly likely, creating a digital edition. Unquestionably, you will need to acquire expertise in a set of fields of intellectual engagement, and your existing knowledge is likely to be unevenly spread among them. They will include the following:

- the nature of early modern theatrical manuscripts;
- the early modern printing press and its features (and quirks);
- the early modern print shop and its processes (and quirks);
- theories of text and textual transmission;
- unfamiliar spelling and punctuation practice;
- early modern playhouses and their features (and quirks);
- performance history, both at the time of your play's first performance and across the period(s), brief or extended, of your play's theatrical afterlife, assuming it has one;
- the cultural, social and political history of the moment of your play's first performances and of its afterlife;
- the critical history of your play – how it has been understood in the past and how the way it is understood has changed across time;
- the critical approaches that are most appropriate for situating the play for your readers, for addressing its challenges and obscurities and for giving your readers a fresh and current understanding of the work the play does.

If you look back at the order in which we presented this list of fields about which an editor must expect to be knowledgeable, you will see that we give away our own biases. We begin with the text, with early printing processes; we end with current criticism. But this is sequence, not division. An editor's critical engagements cannot be detached from the more technical aspects of her editorial work – rather, her critical stance will inform everything she does as an editor. She will need to learn the practical skills of editing, such as recognizing why a verse passage may be mis-set as prose or an entrance may be delayed or anticipated or how, and whether, to combine part lines, but she will need a sound theoretical base too – by which we mean a disciplined perspective on the intellectual premises that inform and underpin each stage of the editing process. The one won't be adequate without the other. And the theoretical base cannot be prescribed. It will be located at the intersection of your own textual and critical interests, orientations and experiences. In other words, who you are as a critic will also be who you are as an editor.

We said that you can only stop editing your play when you have done everything needed. This is true, but it is not sufficient. You do need to stop editing your play at a certain point, and we define that certain point as the submission date you agreed to in your contract. Editing a volume for a scholarly series can lead to a severe reluctance to let go, a belief that the finished product must be nothing less than perfect. But no edition is perfect, and if it takes too many years to edit your play, then your edition will be out of date before it is published. Editions of Shakespeare's plays last about twenty years before they are fairly thoroughly superseded; if you take ten years to create your edition, it may well be out of date in another ten. Editions of other playwrights' work tend to last longer simply because there isn't the same incentive for publishers to replace them, but they will probably begin to look long in the tooth after roughly the same number of years.

Now, a few final notes before we turn to practicalities.

People come to editing early modern texts for the first time down different paths. The most common is the one GM took, being invited to do so by the general editor of a series. Sometimes the path is more like SG's, where the potential editor finds material she thinks should be shared and proposes a publication to some (usually senior) person who is a general editor or otherwise heads a series for an organization such as the Malone Society or the Arizona Center for Medieval and Renaissance Studies or Manchester University Press (for the long-standing Revels series). In addition, undergraduate and graduate students are increasingly being introduced to editing in the classroom, both because it enables them better to understand the edited texts they use and because it forms an intensive reading practice for literature classes. This guide is for anyone who begins to edit, whether professional scholar or student, whether an entire play or a ten-line passage.

We have cited examples from the work of a range of playwrights, including plays we have each edited or are currently editing – Beaumont and Fletcher's *Philaster*, Jonson, Chapman and Marston's *Eastward Ho!*, Marston's *The Wonder of Women, or Sophonisba*, Middleton and Rowley's *A Fair Quarrel* and *The Changeling* – but most often we turn to Shakespeare's plays, and not only the plays we have ourselves edited: *Romeo and Juliet*, *1*

Henry IV, *All's Well That Ends Well*, *Pericles* and *Henry VIII*. We have done this not because we are obsessively canonical (we are both keen advocates for early modern playwrights who aren't Shakespeare, not least his collaborator on three plays, John Fletcher) but simply because the Shakespearean examples are likely to be the most immediately familiar to our readers.

Another point that needs reiterating: the modest word count of an Element precludes comprehensive treatment. We do not have space, for instance, to discuss the editing of poetry or prose, and what we say about drama will unavoidably be very truncated indeed. Similarly, throughout we mention useful sources on everything from print shops to theories of the text, but please note that these citations are, at best, gestural. A fuller list of helpful materials, including everything we mention in this Element, can be found on pp. 93–100. Because of the diversity of approaches to editing and the necessary brevity with which we write, experienced editors and textual scholars may well find cause to take issue with something we say on virtually every page. But brevity has obvious value: a lengthier guide might well be unappealing to the very readers we hope to attract – those editing for the first time, those curious about editing and those who don't plan to edit but want to know what editors do. We suggest that you, the reader, view this Element as being a little like a cookbook, at least in the 'practice' section. It serves essentially as a kind of lengthy recipe: how to cook an edition. But where some cooks follow recipes faithfully, others tend to take their cue from a recipe before modifying it, turning back to the book only for a reminder of certain techniques or a particular combination of ingredients. We hope our readers will feel free to use this Element in any way that works for them.

In the next, longest section – on practice – we will address key aspects of the editing process, describing each briefly and offering a set of examples to clarify the issues. We begin with **terminology**, and then we look in turn at **kinds of edition** and offer suggestions for work that would usefully be done **before you begin** editing. Then we turn to the **order of work** (along with certain underlying theoretical issues that cannot wait for the final section), beginning by addressing **modernization**, **emendation** and **lineation** before discussing the nature and role of **textual notes**, **commentary notes** and the **critical/textual introduction** and offering some **concluding advice**.

Editing an Early Modern Play 9

If you are reading this Element as a first-time editor, we hope you enjoy editing your first play as much as we enjoyed editing ours.

2 Practice

2.1 Terminology

The terminology used by editors to describe their work can be opaque to anyone trying for the first time to develop a sense of what editors do. We therefore open this section on practice with some definitions. But bear in mind that for virtually every term we define here there are alternative meanings and alternative usages, depending both on your position in respect of textual theory and on the series for which you are editing. Bear in mind too that you will find much fuller, more precise definitions in the reading list; our word limit means significant compression is unavoidable here. Your general editor, assuming you have one (or your instructor if you are editing as a classroom exercise), must be your guide in these matters. We deploy terms here in the way we have done for the series we ourselves have general-edited, but we urge you to adapt our terminology to match that used by your own general editors, and at each stage, if there is a choice between what we say and what your general editor says, then always choose the latter. We will expand on each definition later in the chapter, but please remember that we have written this Element with people new to editing in mind, and if some of it seems too obvious (e.g., the difference between quarto and folio), then please skip ahead.

People typically use the term **text** loosely. Claire Bourne notes that 'text' may operate 'as much as a generalized concept ("*the* text"; and even the state of "textuality" itself) as it does as a placeholder for each of the specific material textual forms in which Shakespeare's ... writings persist in the historical record ("*a* text")'.[5] Consequently, in general conversation, 'the text of *Hamlet*' may mean a material form, or it may mean the words that make up the tragedy *Hamlet*. But with early modern plays – not least with

---

[5] Claire M. L. Bourne, Introduction *to Shakespeare/Text: Contemporary Readings in Textual Studies, Editing and Performance* (Bloomsbury Publishing, 2021), p. 1.

Hamlet, for which there are three quite different early printed versions that may be considered in one way or another 'Shakespeare's' – it matters to be more precise. For our purposes in this Element, by **text** we mean printed matter on a page – that is, the words on that page, along perhaps with some of the material features of the printed page (printers' ornaments, say). An **edition**, formally defined, is 'the whole number of copies of a book printed ... from one setting-up of type'; it is also, more broadly, a text that has been intervened in by someone other than the writer, as in 'a Cambridge edition'.[6] The printed text of an early modern play (in most cases, the only form in which the text is available to us) is in fact almost certainly already an edition in the sense that agents other than the playwright have intervened in its production, including typesetters (compositors).[7] You may not wish to call Compositor A or B an *editor* of the Shakespeare First Folio, but you might want to use the term for Ralph Crane, the scribe who prepared several of the plays for printing in the First Folio (the first published collection of Shakespeare's dramatic corpus), imposing in the process his preference for heavy punctuation. Or you might decide that Shakespeare's colleagues John Heminges and Henry Condell are editors, since they brought the volume into existence in collaboration with a syndicate of publishers. Or you may argue that editors only come later in the history of a text.

A **witness** is a material object that exemplifies the text. For Chaucer scholars, there can be seventy or more manuscript witnesses to a single passage; life is much easier for editors of early modern drama, since for a given play there is often only one early printed text, usually a quarto, and no manuscript. The **base text** (also called a copy text) is the early witness you choose to transcribe and edit, one that you believe best represents the play in an authoritative early form and the one from which you will depart (i.e., that you will in some way emend) only if you are convinced it incorporates an error. The question of the base text tends only to become complicated when

---

[6] Ronald B. McKerrow, *An Introduction to Bibliography for Literary Students*, Second Impression (Oxford: Clarendon Press, 1928), p. 175.

[7] See Sonia Massai, *Shakespeare and the Rise of the Editor* (Cambridge University Press, 2007).

a play (*Hamlet*, *Othello* and *King Lear* are the most celebrated instances) exists in more than one potentially authoritative early printed form – 'authoritative' here meaning that direct proximity to a now-lost manuscript, authorial or theatrical, can reasonably be inferred. Sometimes there is only a single surviving witness, as is the case with the unique copy of the first quarto (Q1) of *Titus Andronicus* (1594) at the Folger Shakespeare Library, or there can be eighty-two in one library alone, as with the Folger's collection of First Folios. (A quarto, so called because the sheets of paper are folded in four, is a small book; sheets of a folio are folded in half, forming a larger, usually grander book. If more than one text of a given play was published, they become known as Q1, Q2 or F1, F2, etc. More on this shortly.)

A **crux** (the Latin word for 'cross', arguably overemphasizing the editor's suffering) is a word or passage that, due to a problem of transmission, requires the editor to make a difficult choice. Do not be surprised if you cannot solve every crux satisfactorily.

A **speech prefix** (SP) (sometimes 'speech heading') is the abbreviation used in a play text to identify who is speaking. Compositors could be idiosyncratic in their choice of abbreviation, and speech prefixes could vary a great deal for a single character in a given text – probably the most famous instance of this is Lady Capulet in Q2 *Romeo and Juliet* (1599) whose SP is at different times *Wife*, *Capulets Wife*, *Old Lady* and *Mother*. Omitted or mistaken SPs are an editorial hazard to watch for.

A **stage direction** (SD) is an instruction in the text of a play indicating stage action, such as movement by an actor ('*draws his sword*'), music ('*Infernal music* [*plays*] *softly*' [*Sophonisba*, 4.1][8]) or other performance requirements ('*They pull a piece of Pericles' armour from the net*'[9]). The two most frequent kinds of SDs are **entry directions**, noting the arrival of

---

[8] John Marston, *The Wonder of Women, or Sophonisba*, ed. Suzanne Gossett (Oxford University Press, forthcoming).

[9] Suzanne Gossett, ed., *Pericles* (Bloomsbury Arden Shakespeare, 2004), 2.1.11–16. All citations from Shakespeare in this Element are taken from the New Cambridge editions except for the plays we have edited ourselves, i.e., for GM *Henry VIII* and for SG *Pericles* and *All's Well that Ends Well*, all published in the Arden Shakespeare third series.

a character on stage, and **exit directions**, noting a character's departure from the stage. Early printed play texts frequently omit one or the other of these, so an editor must pay particular attention to the movement of characters on and off stage and supply necessary directions if a character speaks yet has apparently not entered or who has been described as having departed. Anything an editor adds to the base text to elucidate the action – the marking of an aside or the expansion of an original stage direction – should be enclosed within **square brackets** (as we did with '[*plays*]' in the citation from *Sophonisba* just now, where the base text has the slightly cryptic SD '*Infernal music softly*', and the editor has added '*plays*' to clarify). It never ceases to amaze instructors that students mostly don't realize that anything in square brackets on the page they are reading should be treated as an offer of assistance to the reader by the editor, not as the playwright's own instruction. As a rule of thumb, this assistance can be viewed as giving the reader information that a theatre audience would obtain by viewing the stage action.

A **textual note** (TN) is a highly compressed record of an intervention in the text, whether first made by the current editor or by a prior editor. In a full critical edition, you will be expected to supply a textual note every time your edition varies significantly from your base text, and you may have a commentary note explaining your decision to emend or not to emend. In most cases, 'significantly' means that the notes will indicate *words* you have **emended** (i.e., changed in some way so as to correct an error or for some other reason you can defend), but if changing the *punctuation* or modernizing *spelling* changes the meaning, then you will also record the change. Occasionally, a textual note will include an alternative emendation (perhaps one suggested by another editor) that you find plausible and think worth noting for the reader but do not yourself adopt.

A **commentary note** (CN) is designed to explain something that might otherwise not be understood by the reader, including definitions of early modern words, classical and Biblical references, proverbial language, brief sections of the source materials, historical context or the way particular moments were performed in a landmark production. A CN is necessarily brief, but it is not compressed to the point of near-incomprehensibility as a TN is. There is an art to writing a good CN. An enjoyable challenge, once you have created as brief a CN as is necessary to explain a point, is then to try to remove a further five or ten words without losing the sense.

In some contexts, editors are asked to provide **glossarial notes** (or **glosses**) rather than, or in addition to, CNs. These usually offer very brief (one- or two-word) definitions of early modern words or phrases that are likely to need explaining for the reader.

Conversely, some series will permit **longer notes** or **appendices** to address issues that ramify beyond a commentary note, though these still require very concise writing. There should be as few longer notes as possible, not least because any commentary-related material deferred to the end of an edition is *far* less likely to be read than are commentary notes on the same page as the relevant text. Much longer discussion, including of the text, belongs in the general introduction.

This is enough terminology for now. More will appear as we write, but we thought it best to begin by defining a few basics. Basics they may be, but they each raise issues over which textual editors have argued vehemently for centuries.

2.2 What Kind of Edition Are You Producing?

For the purposes of this Element, we are making certain assumptions about the kind of edition you are creating.

- We are assuming that, like most editions today, yours is to be a modern-spelling edition – a transformation that can be considerably more complex than it seems. Some editors, it is worth noting, consider a modern-spelling edition to be too compromised a reproduction of an early modern text, and we respect this stance; we are, however, more pragmatic in our approach, believing in a politics, and a pedagogy, of accessibility.[10]

---

[10] The other main editorial options are a 'diplomatic' edition, a highly scholarly edition that reproduces all the orthographic information of the base text (spelling, punctuation, lineation, marginalia), a mode now arguably superseded by digital 'hypertext' editions that present more information than is possible on a printed page and may, for instance, offer pop-up textual notes or access to alternative texts; a 'semi-diplomatic' edition, which reproduces a select number, rather than all, of the original features of the text; an 'original-spelling' edition, which reproduces the spelling and accidentals (punctuation, capitalization, etc.) of the base text but may perform conservative emendation while providing the apparatus of a critical

- We are assuming that you have been asked to edit for a series that has a general editor. We are assuming, too, that the series has norms and methods expressed in a set of guidelines. You will be expected to adjust your modernized spelling and punctuation to the publisher's norms. Currently, given the locations of the principal publishers of early modern play texts, these norms are likely to be those either of the US or the UK or, sometimes, Canada. By signing up to the series you have agreed to adopt these norms, which may require you to alter your own 'natural' practices, including of punctuation. This will affect not only apparently 'mechanical' issues such as the placement of quotation marks before or after the comma but also meaningful issues such as the frequency and placement of commas as markers of, say, subordinate clauses. Series guidelines can vary widely in extent: those for the Arden Shakespeare Fourth Series are around fifty pages in length, while those for the New Variorum Shakespeare clock in at just under two hundred!
- We are assuming that there is no surviving early manuscript of your play, as is almost always the case.[11] Consequently, you will be working from a printed base text, and the nature of the manuscript from which it was printed can only be inferred from that printed text.
- We are assuming that you have been commissioned to produce not only a text but a complete critical edition containing all the usual apparatus – textual notes, commentary notes, introduction – as well, possibly, as appendices that are either particularly pertinent or required by the series guidelines.

Before you begin, you need to think carefully about your expected **readers**. This, as we noted in the preface, is the single most important

---

edition. As an example, *Jacobean Academic Plays*, ed. Suzanne Gossett and Thomas L. Berger (Malone Society Collections, 1988), is a 'diplomatic edition' of Folger manuscript J.a.1, maintaining original spelling, lineation, abbreviations and notes for such matters as interlineations. The Malone Society has since replaced such editions with photographs of the textual witnesses.

[11] William B. Long notes that there are 'precious few' surviving English manuscript playbooks, 'eighteen ... out of probably 3,000'. See '" Precious Few": English Manuscript Playbooks', in *A Companion to Shakespeare*, ed. David Scott Kastan (Wiley, 1999), pp. 414–433 (414).

question for an editor. It is crucial that you keep your readers in mind throughout the editing process and that you provide them with everything necessary to help them understand and enjoy the play. Will these readers, for instance, be students completing pre-university education, for whom more than a brief history of the text might be disconcerting, even off-putting, and who might need considerable help envisioning the action? Or will yours be an edition intended for general readers? Or for scholars of the author or the period who would like as much information as possible and will already have acquired a good deal of knowledge about the period, the theatrical scene and critical history? Or is it to be used by acting companies, who may dislike the very stage directions you insert to aid students in visualizing the play but which seem to limit possibilities for an actor or director? The answer to these questions will determine a great deal about the editing task you are undertaking.

The second question you need to ask yourself about the work you are doing for your readers is more technical. **What kind of** text do you want your edition to provide? A direct reproduction of the base text with all its flaws and limitations? An eclectic text, that is, one that irons out flaws and misprints by emending from various sources, whether alternative printings such as subsequent quartos or editorial inspiration? Do you aim for a text as it originally came from the playwright's pen, as you believe on the basis of your understanding of the printing process and thus of the missing manuscript from which your base text was printed? Or, to shift perspective, are you editing a text not as it was written by the playwright but as it was presented at a particular performance? These are fundamental choices, and your answer will affect most subsequent decisions you make as you create your edition. This said, it may be that the choice has in fact been determined in advance for your series, in which case you will need to make your peace with it.

2.3 Before You Begin

Before you begin editing the play you have been assigned, we urge you to take the time to do four things:

- **Read, or re-read, your playwright's work**, and fill in gaps in your familiarity with early modern drama in general, especially (1) plays by

playwrights who may have collaborated with yours, (2) plays performed by the same acting company and (3) plays first performed around the time of your play's first performance.[12]
- **Fill in gaps in your familiarity with the critical field.** Depending on the play you are editing – one by, for example, John Day or Thomas May – you may be able to read all the criticism in a few days. Most of the time, given how much criticism has been written about many early modern plays, you will need to find triaging principles to determine the most significant lines of critical thought about your play, both historically and in the present moment.
- Introduce yourself, if you have not already done so, to **early modern handwriting**, especially secretary hand (the standard mode of handwriting of the period).[13] (See Figure 1.)
- Introduce yourself, if you have not already done so, to **the printing process** in the early modern period, including the logistics of typesetting and the mechanics of the wooden hand printing press.[14]

---

[12] The most accessible source for this information is Alan B. Farmer and Zachary Lesser's *Database of Early English Playbooks* (DEEP): https://deepplaybooks.org/.

[13] A useful book on early modern handwriting is Jean F. Preston and Laetitia Yaendle, *English Handwriting 1400–1650: An Introductory Manual* (Pegasus Press, 1999). Helpful websites include the Folger's Practical Paleography wiki (http://folgerpedia.folger.edu/Practical Paleography) and an online tutorial offered by the UK's National Archives (https://webarchive.nationalarchives.gov.uk/ukgwa/20230801144244/https://www.nationalarchives.gov.uk/palaeography/).

[14] See, for instance, Sarah Werner, *Studying Early Printed Books, 1450–1800: A Practical Guide* (Wiley, 2019) and her highly informative website www.earlyprintedbooks.com/; Mark Bland, *A Guide to Early Printed Books and Manuscripts* (Wiley-Blackwell, 2010); and Laurie E. Maguire, 'The Craft of Printing (1600)', in *A Companion to Shakespeare*, ed. David Scott Kastan (Wiley Blackwell, 1999). There are also helpful images in McKerrow, *An Introduction*, and in Philip Gaskell's indispensable, *A New Introduction to Bibliography* (Oxford University Press, 1972).

Editing an Early Modern Play 17

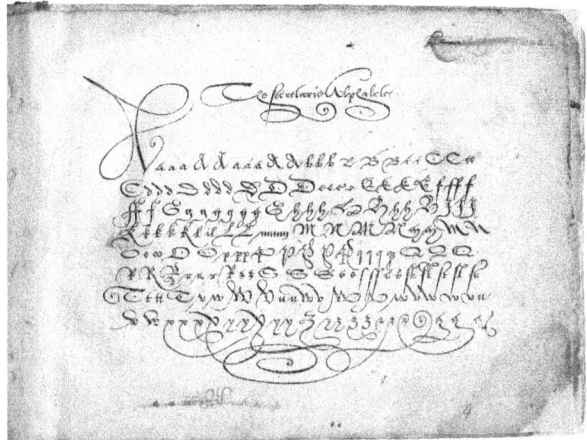

Figure 1 Jehan de Beau-Chesne, *A booke containing diuers sortes of hands: as well the English as French secretarie with the Italian, Roman, chancelry and court hands* (London: Richard Field, 1602), STC 6450.2, plate 4, reproduced by kind permission of the Folger Shakespeare Library

A little more on these last two points. While we do not have space here to offer a tutorial on how to read secretary hand or on early modern printing processes, we would urge you, if you have not already had some training in these areas, to acquaint yourself with both. You don't have to become a wholly fluent reader of secretary hand, nor do you have to be able effortlessly to reconstruct each stage of the printing process, but acquiring a working knowledge of the way early modern people formed their letters when writing and of the way early modern printers produced play texts will be indispensable for your editing experience. In truth, you should not begin to edit before you have absorbed the rudiments of both, simply because understanding some of the most basic issues of your text will require awareness of the ease, for instance, with which secretary hand 'c' and 't' can be mixed up by someone reading a careless hand or with which an error in the casting-off process (we will explain casting-off in due course) can affect the printed text you are editing.

Why does this knowledge matter so much? The answer is a practical one that also takes you directly into the theoretical heart of the business of editing. Practically, the problem that faces all editors of early modern plays is the fragmentary and mostly secondary nature of what has survived over four hundred years – that is, when we edit an early modern play we are working not from a neatly written final manuscript as it was handed to the acting company by the playwright(s) but from a printed text, most often a quarto, based on a lost manuscript of some kind, not necessarily either neat or final, and produced by a process that inevitably introduced both variation and error in a range of ways. We say 'manuscript of some kind' because the evidence suggests that sometimes a play was printed from the playwright's (or playwrights') rough, perhaps draft, script (traditionally known as 'foul papers'), designed to be copied out neatly a bit later; sometimes from a carefully copied-out script (a 'fair copy', made either by the playwright or by an acting company's scribe); sometimes from a manuscript that appeared to be a mixture of the playwright's writing and annotations by someone else, for example, the 'bookkeeper', preparing for a stage presentation and thinking about the practicalities of performance. (Textual scholars are wary of the loaded binary 'fair'/ 'foul'; see Section 3.) But mostly we don't have these manuscripts, nor do we have the scholar's holy grail: a play text that exists both in manuscript and in an early printed quarto that would enable us to see what a professional compositor did with a playwright's or a theatre company's manuscript. (It is especially infuriating for Shakespearean textual scholars that while most scholars now agree that we have an instance of a play manuscript in Shakespeare's hand – a scene or two in *Sir Thomas More* – the play was never printed in the period.) As a result, editors are forced to infer the nature of the manuscript of their play from the printed text that has survived. This is why the editor needs to know a certain amount both about early modern handwriting and about the printing process, and why editorial practice can never be separated from theory.

The principal book formats with which editors of early modern plays are likely to work are quartos and folios. If you are editing a play from a printed

Editing an Early Modern Play 19

Figure 2 A completed forme with type and furniture, reproduced by kind permission of Joshua Eckhardt, Jamie Mahoney, and their fall 2022 book history students at Virginia Commonwealth University

text, most often you will be editing from a quarto; the exceptions are plays in the Jonson, Shakespeare and 'Beaumont and Fletcher' canons, which were published (sometimes exclusively) in the larger, multi-play folio format – Jonson's with his direct involvement, the others after their lifetimes. To understand the printing process, it helps to understand certain terms, including, for instance, **forme** and **sheet**, so we will now offer some brief definitions. The **sheet** is the paper that was printed and folded to form the basic unit of a book. The early modern paper sheet was, very roughly, what we would now call A3

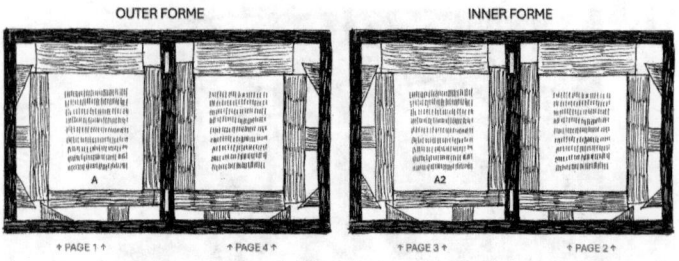

Figure 3 A diagram of inner and outer formes, reproduced by kind permission of Claire M. L. Bourne

size (cut down the middle of the longer side, it thus becomes, again very roughly, A4 or US letter size). A **forme** is what you get when you ('you' being the **compositor**) arrange the metal type within a wooden frame in the appropriate way for your chosen page size, then fill the spaces with lengths of wood (called **furniture**), and finally lock it all into place by gently hammering in wedges with a mallet. (See Figure 2.) Depending on the format you have chosen, you will set up your formes as an outer and an inner forme, meaning that you will print your sheet on one side from the outer forme and on the other from the inner forme, and you will then fold the paper so that the side printed from the latter is on the inside. (See Figure 3.) The folding is what produces the format. A **quarto** is made up of full-size sheets of paper folded twice, once across and once lengthwise. With the top fold cut open, this yields a set of four leaves or eight pages. A **folio** is made by folding full size sheets of paper once and nesting them one inside the other, in the case of the Shakespeare First Folio in groups of three. For a quarto, each group of eight pages constituted one **gathering** (or **quire** or, sometimes, **signature**), with the **recto** or right-hand pages marked at the bottom in the A gathering A – the 1 was invariably omitted – A2, A3 and A4. (The fourth and last of these pages tends to have no mark because it is the final leaf in the gathering and is implied by the other three; for the bookbinder, once the first three leaves are in the correct position, the fourth will necessarily also be correct. If you need to cite this page, then do so by way of the implied signature.) The **verso** or left-hand page was not marked, but the identification for the page of an early book may read, for example, 'A4^v', that is, the reverse side of page A4. For a quarto, a normal running order of signature marks might therefore resemble, A[1^r], [A1^v], A2[^{r}], [A2^v], A3[^{r}], [A3^v], [A4^r], [A4^v], B[1^r], [B1^v], B2[^{r}] and so on, but the convention in citations is to supply the signature marks whether or not they are actually printed (i.e., A1^r, A1^v and so on). For the Shakespeare First Folio, which is what is known as a 'folio in sixes', each gathering would consist of three sheets of paper, forming six leaves and thus twelve pages. Signature markings (A4^r, B3^v, etc.) are more important bibliographically than page numbers because they make visible the way in which the book has been assembled and because, as often as not, page numbering in early modern printed texts goes awry (try following the page numbers through the Shakespeare First Folio, and you will soon see the problem). Generally, you should cite the signature, not the page number, when you refer to an early modern printed text.

We do not have space to say more here – and others, not least Gaskell, do so better and far more precisely – but our point is that it is essential for the first-time editor to acquire awareness of the printing formats of early modern plays, of the printing practices expressed by those formats and of the impact of those practices on editing. We will address a few instances of visible errors in the printed text that result (1) from a **compositor** (typesetter) misreading secretary hand, and (2) from print house problems such as miscalculations in **casting off** manuscript copy. But first it might be helpful to discuss the roles in the print shop.

Figure 4 is an image of an early seventeenth-century Flemish print shop that shows the various tasks being performed in much the same way they would have been in London: To the left are two **compositors** setting type from typecases, using (though it is not obvious in this image) a composing stick to hold a few lines of type and then transferring them to a galley, from which the **forme** would be set. A colleague is pointing at the **manuscript copy**, pinned to the wall, from which they are working, perhaps addressing queries about the handwriting. In the foreground is a print worker who may also be composing or may be returning type to the typecase, which is arranged in two parts: boxes in half of the top hold 'upper case' letters or majuscules alphabetically, boxes in the other half of the top hold various

Figure 4 Jan van der Straet, *Impressio librorum Ioan*. ([Antwerp]: Phls. Galle excud, [ca. 1591]), ART Vol. f81 no.4, plate 4, reproduced by kind permission of the Folger Shakespeare Library

symbols, while boxes of various sizes in the lower half hold 'lower-case' letters or minuscules, arranged with the 'types in most frequent use being towards the centre where they are handiest for the compositor'.[15] (For an illustration of a typecase, see Figure 5.) Behind him a colleague with spectacles is presumably proofreading a printed sheet. In the centre, a boy, perhaps learning the trade as an apprentice (a 'printer's devil', as he would have been known), seems to be comparing a printed sheet to the forme from which it was printed or is stacking paper, while behind him a worker is inking a forme. To the right, the hand press is in action, printing a sheet (instances of printed sheets are drying on a line above the printer's head), while a person who is presumably the printer is overseeing proceedings. (A printer was, as it

---

[15] McKerrow, *An Introduction*, p. 8.

Editing an Early Modern Play 23

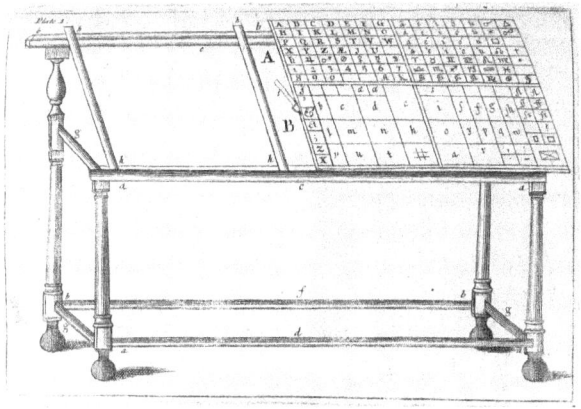

Figure 5 Joseph Moxon, *Mechanick Exercises; Or the Doctrine of Handy-Works. Applied to the Art of Printing* (London: for Joseph Moxon, 1683), RB 138367, reproduced by kind permission of Huntington Library

happens, by no means always a man, given that widows and daughters regularly inherited print shops.[16]) The overall sense is of a dedicated team, each member of which knows their task and is operating collaboratively and professionally.

To turn, then, to examples of problems in the text and their likely origin in print house practice. First, an example of **compositorial misreading** of manuscript copy. We have already mentioned that in secretary hand certain letters – e and o, c and t, and others – can be hard to distinguish. In *Hamlet*, in the text of the second quarto (1604), Laertes promises that he will open his arms to his dead father Polonius's friends 'and like the kind life-rendring Pelican / Repast them with my blood' (L1^v).[17] But the Folio instead has him promising to do this 'like the kinde

---

[16] See Molly Yarn, *Shakespeare's 'Lady Editors': A New History of the Shakespearean Text* (Cambridge University Press, 2022).

[17] *Hamlet*, ed. by Philip Edwards, rev. by Heather Hirschfeld, The New Cambridge Shakespeare (Cambridge University Press, 2019), pp. 146–147.

Life-rend'ring Politician' (TLN 2896). Often the Folio improves on the early quartos, but in this case the myth of the self-sacrificial pelican (supposed in classical times suicidally to peck its own breast to produce blood for its chicks to feed on; the bird subsequently became a type of Christ) is clearly intended. How could such an error – clearly not a correction but a misreading of an independent manuscript – happen? If the playwright spelled 'Pellican' with two l's (as the *Oxford English Dictionary* shows was the most familiar spelling up to and throughout the seventeenth century) and his secretary-hand forms of e and o, and c and t, are sloppy (as Shakespeare's, to judge from Hand D of *Sir Thomas More*, seem to have been), then the compositor's error becomes comprehensible.

Secondly, an example of an error in **casting off**. Casting off is the term for one of the printer's preliminary tasks, especially when setting by forme, which is to calculate how many written lines will fit on the page he is going to print and to make a mark on the manuscript after a certain number of lines to guide the compositor setting the type. Errors in casting off arise when the printer miscalculates the amount of text required for each page of a quarto or folio. To understand how errors arose in casting off for a quarto, take a sheet of paper, fold it twice but don't cut it, insert the signature indications from A1^r to A4^v, and open it. Now you will see that each side of the sheet will hold four pages' worth of printed text. Textual analysts, recognizing the process of 'setting by formes', refer to the side that begins with A1^r as 'A outer' and the side that begins with A1^v as 'A inner': when folded, the latter will be on the inside. Because these pages are not consecutive – printers rarely set *seriatim*, that is, in page-by-page order, because doing so required using a good deal more type – if the compositor runs out of space, he cannot simply push a few words on to the next page; he has no choice but to make the words before the mark that indicates the end of the page fit into the space available.

Figure 6 shows lines of apparent prose on D4^r of quarto (Q) *King Lear*, published in 1608. Editors of Q *King Lear*, prompted (probably by the layout of the same speech in the First Folio text of the play) to recognize the

Editing an Early Modern Play 25

> ganted by the noy...
> *Glost*, Let him flie farre not in this land shall hee remaine vn-caught and found, dispatch, the noble Duke my maister, my worthy Arch and Patron, comes to night, by his authoritie I will proclaime it, that he which finds him shall deserue our thankes, bringing the murderous caytife to the stake, hee that conceals him, death.
> *B.A.* When I disswaded him from his intent, and found him

Figure 6 William Shakespeare, Q King Lear D4^r – STC 22292 copy 1, reproduced by kind permission of Folger Shakespeare Library

pattern of versification in these lines, normally represent them something like this:

> Let him fly far;
> Not in this land shall he remain uncaught,
> And, found, dispatch. The noble Duke, my master,
> My worthy arch and patron, comes tonight:
> By his authority I will proclaim it
> That he which finds him shall deserve our thanks,
> Bringing the murderous caitiff to the stake.
> He that conceals him, death!

Why do these verse lines appear set out as prose in Q *King Lear*? The *Lear* quarto was, it seems, the first play printed by a printer called Nicholas Okes, and he did not find it easy. As the Arden Shakespeare Third Series editor notes: 'it was very badly printed by two compositors, one probably an apprentice, and neither notable for competence'.[18] It looks as if the compositor setting these lines found he had too much text remaining for the space available and had no choice but to compress verse into prose so that the end of signature D and the beginning of signature E could connect properly. Or, as Peter Blayney has suggested, it may have come about because Okes, not accustomed to printing drama, was short

---

[18] *King Lear*, ed. R. A. Foakes, The Arden Shakespeare Third Series (Bloomsbury Publishing, 1997), p. 120.

Figure 7 William Shakespeare, Q1 *Romeo and Juliet* F2ʳ – STC 22322, reproduced by kind permission of Folger Shakespeare Library

of the spacing material he needed to fill out the lines when text was set as verse and hence resorted to prose.[19]

Pages can, by contrast, be suspiciously empty, showing a great deal of white space for no obvious reason. Figure 7 shows Q1 *Romeo and Juliet* (1597) F2ʳ. It looks as if the compositor has found himself in the opposite position from his counterpart setting Q *Lear*. In this instance, an error of casting off has meant that he has too *few* lines of text to take him to the end of F2ʳ, so he has inserted low-profile spacing material to fill out the page. Another technique compositors deployed in this situation was to create verse from prose to use up more page space. Figure 8, a passage from Q *Henry V*, is an example of prose set as rough verse. Note how the first word of each line is capitalized.

---

[19] Peter W. M. Blayney, *The Texts of King Lear and Their Origins*, vol. 1: *Nicholas Okes and the First Quarto* (Cambridge University Press, 1982), p. 144.

> *Kin.* Captain *Flewellen,* when *Alonson* and I was
> Downe together, *I* tooke this gloue off from his helmet,
> Here *Flewellen,* weare it. *If* any do challenge it,
> He is a friend of *Alonsons,*
> And an enemy to mee.
>   *Fle.* Your maieſtie doth me as great a fauour
> As can be deſired in the harts of his ſubiects,
> *I* would ſee that man now that ſhould chalenge this gloue:
> And it pleaſe God of his grace, *I* would but ſee him,
> That is all.
>   *Kin.* *Flewellen* know'ſt thou Captaine *Gower?*
>   *Fle.* Captaine *Gower* is my friend.
> And if it like your maieſtie, *I* know him very well,
>   *Kin.* Go call him hither.
>   *Flew.* *I* will and it ſhall pleaſe your maieſtie,
>   *Kin.* Follow *Flewellen* cloſely at the heeles,
> The gloue he weares, it was the ſouldiers:
>   F 2   *It.*

Figure 8 William Shakespeare, Q1 *Henry V* F2^r – RB 69321, reproduced by kind permission of Huntington Library

An editor, editing Q *Henry V* and prompted by the layout of most of these lines as prose in the First Folio text of the play, might represent these lines thus:

King Henry	Captain Llewelyn, when Alençon and I was down together, I took this glove off from his helmet. Here, Llewelyn, wear it. If any do challenge it, he is a friend of Alençon's and an enemy to me.
Llewelyn	Your majesty doth me as great a favour as can be desired in the hearts of his subjects. I would see that man now that should challenge this glove, an it please God of his grace. I would but see him, that is all.
King Henry	Llewelyn, know'st thou Captain Gower?
Llewelyn	Captain Gower is my friend and, if it like your majesty, I know him very well.
King Henry	Go call him hither.
Llewelyn	I will, an it shall please your majesty. [*Exit.*]
King Henry	[*to the Lords*]
	Follow Llewelyn closely at the heels;
	The glove he wears, it was the soldier's.

In other words, the editor treats the passage as prose, not verse, up to the King's speech to the lords.

Finally, here is an example of another kind of error: a **turned letter**. (This term may well be a misnomer. Compositors setting type would automatically feel for the slot at the bottom of a piece of type and align it accordingly; thus a 'turned letter' is more likely to be the result of 'foul case', that is, type – 'n' and 'u' in this example – being returned to the wrong box in the typecase.) The Countess in *All's Well That Ends Well* confronts Helen and explains that now she has discovered the root of her strange behaviour, which she describes as 'The mistrie of your louelinesse', a phrase that, although it is correct English and might seem to the compositor to make sense, does not fit the situation of the two women (see Figure 9). The sense becomes coherent, however, when the 'u' is imagined upside down, as the correct 'n'; Helen has been keeping herself apart, in her 'l**o**neliness', to think about her love. Similar foul case occurs in the 1620 quarto of Beaumont and Fletcher's *Philaster*, which has the villain 'shake like a true truant' instead of, as in the 1622 'good' quarto, 'shake like a true tenant', and most famously recurs in *Othello*, as we will see in the next section.

An editor who is aware of print house processes can use this knowledge to help make decisions about her text. In the case of *All's Well*, an editor might decide that 'loveliness' is a defensible reading, despite its apparent obscurity, and stick with it, or she may decide on the basis of the 'foul case' to emend to 'loneliness' – a reading that both creates clearer sense and is defensible on a bibliographical basis. Equally, an editor of Q *Lear*, working

> God shield you meane it not, daughter and mother
> So striue vpon your pulse; vvhat pale agen?
> My feare hath catcht your fondnesse! now I see
> The mistrie of your louelinesse, and finde
> Your salt teares head, now to all sence 'tis grosse:
> You loue my sonne inuention is asham'd

Figure 9 William Shakespeare, F *All's Well that Ends Well* TLN 495-499 – RBD EL SH15M 1623, reproduced by kind permission of the Free Library of Philadelphia, Rare Book Department

with two items of evidence – the fact that the Folio text sets as consistent verse the lines set out in Q as prose, combined with the demonstrable tendency of compositors to deal with errors of casting off by making verse into prose or vice versa – is likely to set the lines as verse and provide a TN to note what she has done and (probably) a CN to explain the choice. These decisions, in the end, are the editor's, but they must be informed by awareness of the kinds of error that could readily emerge from a lapse in the process somewhere in the print house.[20]

There is, we should add, nothing to match actual hands-on experience to make the processes we have been outlining here come alive. We would encourage the first-time editor to learn, and to try out writing, secretary-hand letter forms, something that can be done most easily by taking one of the online courses provided by libraries including the British Library, the Folger and the Beinecke. Equally, if you are fortunate enough to have access, by way of a library or museum, to a hand press (it doesn't have to be a replica early modern press; time spent with a nineteenth-century iron hand press, for instance, would teach you the basics perfectly well) and have a go yourself at setting and inking type and printing a sheet or two, then this will make all the difference in the world to your understanding of the professional practice of the printers who produced your base text and of the issues they addressed every time they created a book.

2.4 Order of Work

You have now done the necessary preliminary work. So where do you begin the task of editing? In this section, we will answer this and subsequent questions practically, but it is crucial to remember that every decision you make – for starters, what kind of edition you are going to prepare – is underpinned by an intellectual position. While your answer to such questions might seem purely pragmatic – that is, this is what the publisher wants,

---

[20] Two brief accounts of the printing practices and processes for early modern plays are Tiffany Stern, 'From Stage to Printing House', in *Making Shakespeare: From Stage to Page* (Routledge, 2004), pp. 137–158, and Suzanne Gossett, 'The progress of an early modern play', in *Shakespeare and Textual Theory* (Bloomsbury Arden Shakespeare, 2022), pp. 12–22.

this is the form used throughout the series, etc. – there is a lengthy history of debate about the possible answers.

You begin with the **base text**, that is, the early authoritative witness on which you will base your edition.[21] How do you choose your base text? If there is only one surviving text, as for those Shakespeare plays found only in the Folio, or for a Dekker play in an early quarto, or for Shakespeare and Fletcher's *The Two Noble Kinsmen*, published in quarto for the first time in 1634, the choice is made for you. This said, even apparently single-text plays may have a second issue, a reprinting that for the most part uses the original printed sheets but includes changes either in arrangement or in content. New material may be only a few words on the title-page – Marston's name, for instance, was eliminated from some quartos – or as much as a new scene, as in Middleton and Rowley's *A Fair Quarrel*. Your base text is, as we have noted, the witness you choose as your exemplar of the text you are editing, the one you will transcribe and edit. It is important to realize that you will be editing one particular copy of that base text. Your first task, therefore, is to find a copy, very likely by way of *Early English Books Online* (*EEBO*) or possibly a printed facsimile of the original, such as those found in *Shakespeare Plays in Quarto* or the Norton facsimile of the First Folio, if you have access to these volumes.[22] Normally a facsimile is a reproduction of one exemplar, but for the Norton Facsimile Charlton Hinman chose what he considered each 'best' page from the many First Folios in the Folger Shakespeare Library. In scholarly editing you may be

---

[21] This is often called 'copy text', a term coined by R. B. McKerrow and subsequently deployed by W. W. Greg in his field-defining 1950 essay 'The Rationale of Copy-Text' to establish a clear distinction between 'substantive' elements in the text, defined as 'those that affect the author's meaning', and 'accidentals' such as spelling and punctuation. We prefer 'base text' as a neutral term that does not necessarily imply endorsement of Greg's binary, which – groundbreaking as it undoubtedly was – has subsequently been subject to much debate. See Greg, 'The Rationale of Copy Text', *Studies in Bibliography* 3 (1950): 19–36 (21).

[22] *Shakespeare Plays in Quarto*, eds. Michael J. B. Allen and Kenneth Muir (University of California Press, 1981), and *The First Folio of Shakespeare: The Norton Facsimile*, ed. Charlton Hinman (W.W. Norton & Company, 1968; reissued 1996).

expected similarly to collate several copies of your base text to check for printing differences, which occur because, even though early printed sheets were proofed, those containing errors were nevertheless bound into copies of the book.

Your base text would traditionally be defined as the best available instance of a printed text that you believe is closest in line of descent from the manuscript, a premise derived originally from practice in nineteenth-century editing of the Bible. At that time the recapturing of authorial intention was the primary editorial ideal, even if in seeking to do so the editor, by conflating multiple early versions of a text, would produce something different from any single early printed version of that text. Developments in editorial theory and practice in the late twentieth and twenty-first centuries – and in particular developments in the theory and practice of editing *theatrical* texts – now mean that your base text may, for instance, be one that you believe represents the play not as the playwright first wrote it – which you may decide is impossible to ascertain – but in the form it took at a particular moment of early performance. The point, in practical terms, is that you will be editing the base text, not something abstract you might think of as 'the play'.

Once you have chosen your base text, your first move will be to transcribe it. For the purposes of this Element, we are assuming you are working in a standard word-processing programme such as Microsoft Word, though you may be preparing a text for a digital edition – digital is, after all, not only the future of editing, it is its present – and transcribing your text into an encoding language. (Given how rapidly technology changes, naming these languages would probably make this book look dated sooner than anything else.[23]) If so, we assume you will be given specific directions. Don't hesitate to ask questions about method and sustainability, as a challenge for digital texts to date has been the pace with which platforms change or the host withdraws from covering the costs of maintaining the site. No matter whether you are working in Word or in, say, an XML editor, we strongly advise you to transcribe the text yourself (and to save it repeatedly). There is no way to get closer to your text, and in

---

[23] For a discussion of this issue, see 'Textual Studies after the Digital Turn', in Gossett, *Shakespeare and Textual Studies*, pp. 215–227.

our experience having someone else transcribe it is an invitation to error. If, however, you do obtain the text already transcribed, we urge you to **collate** it word for word with your base text. What is **collation**? Collation is the comparison of your text to another – either to the early modern text, say, a quarto, that you are modernizing or, for a different purpose, to previous editions. You may also collate copies of your base text. While transcribing, watch in particular for missing short words ('to', 'the', even 'I') as it is only too easy to have a phrase in your mind and drop one of these as you enter text. This is the same problem that early modern compositors faced as they read a manuscript line and began reaching for the metal type in the typecase. As we just saw, *they* made errors, and *you* will make errors – everybody does – and you need to accept this and keep checking and checking.

We recommend that you create two files, one the initial transcription – to which you will repeatedly refer and which you never alter unless you find a transcription error – and the other your working transcription on which you begin the process of **modernization**.[24] In general, it is best to modernize before you start to emend or to add stage directions. Keep a file of the places where modernizing makes you want to emend but start by modernizing word for word. We would encourage you to have a multiscreen set-up if you can so as to make it as easy as possible to view together, or quickly switch between, several files: your base text, your unmodernized text file, your modernized text file, your textual notes file, and your commentary notes file. (It is useful to make provisional notes towards your commentary as you go along, not least in discussing textual issues that affect meaning or interpretation.) Set out your modernized text file as closely as you can in format to a normal page in the edition or series for which you are editing. Do *not* assume that a copy editor will eventually impose the formatting specified in the series guidelines. If you are told in the series guidelines that you are to place lines of verse below a speech prefix but to place prose on the same line as a speech prefix, then do so consistently from the beginning. This will save endless headaches later.

---

[24] We recommend this as our own preferred practice. Some editors establish the text in old spelling before modernizing, but while that may make the source of errors clearer, we believe it distracts from the need for full modernization.

Try not to look at other editions of your play until you are quite far along. This, we know, is nigh on impossible. Nobody has a will of iron, and many smart people will have already faced, and possibly solved, the challenges you encounter. But try to avoid letting earlier editions instruct you. At the same time, you don't need to reinvent the wheel. Just avoid overdependence on prior editions. If you are editing a play for a series that has had an earlier incarnation (e.g., one of the earlier 'New' Cambridge Shakespeare editions), then you need *both* to avoid overdependence on the work of your immediate predecessor *and* to avoid being too determined to do everything differently: your predecessor may, after all, have had some superb insights, even if in other ways the edition grows out of different editorial premises.

Remember that your edited text will not begin with the play title or the opening entry direction. Preceding it, you should (series guidelines permitting) provide the **paratext** of the base text, which might include, depending on the nature of the quarto or folio you have chosen as your base text, a statement of the fictional location of the action, epistles to the reader, dedicatory verses and perhaps a list of the early modern actors who first, or subsequently, played the major parts, called 'The Names of the Actors' in the First Folio. And, whether or not your base text includes a paratextual cast of characters, you will provide a modernized **List of Roles**, typically differentiated by typeface into speaking and non-speaking roles, usually with accompanying CNs explaining names, places, social positions and so forth, that you determine will be helpful to the reader. Following the text of the play, you will provide appendices as you judge they are needed, or as the series guidelines specify, which may include possible notation for the **music** in the play, passages of **source materials** too lengthy to include in CNs, and perhaps a **doubling chart** showing the multiple roles a given actor might have been able to play and thus the minimum number of actors required for performance.

2.5 Modernization

If you are to make an early modern play accessible for the twenty-first-century reader, you will need to modernize the spelling and punctuation of your text. For the editorial purist this may be anathema, but if you want your edition to be read by more than a handful of scholarly readers, and especially if you want colleagues to be able to use it in the classroom, modernization is a necessary move. (The well-intentioned, rigorously old-spelling but visually rather forbidding *Dramatic Works in the Beaumont and Fletcher Canon*, published with textual, but not critical, apparatus, unfortunately had the unintended effect of limiting readership for the canon in question.[25])

The first thing to remember as you begin the modernizing process is that any meaningful changes you make to your base text must be recorded, and any oddities in the text or your choice of emendation must be explained. This means that, no matter how tedious it might be, you *must* make a note of every change you make, every emended word, altered or inserted stage direction, change of speech prefix or modernization (including of emended words) that is not entirely straightforward. You do not need to record a change of punctuation unless you believe it alters the meaning. In the end, your textual notes and your commentary notes will not discuss everything; no edition can, or should, ever be lengthy enough to discuss everything, not least because discussing everything will only make it harder for the reader to understand which issues are important. But to begin with, as you modernize and, in the process, get to know the features, the quirks, of your base text, it is best to record every move you make (not least so that you don't hate yourself later when you can't remember why you made a particular change).

The issue of modernization has long been a fraught one. In general, modernization means adjusting the spelling and the punctuation of your text to contemporary norms, at the simplest level regularizing long s, u/v and i/j to modern usage (early modern readers did not distinguish between these pairs of letters as English speakers in the twenty-first century do). Note, though, that modernization of early modern English does *not* mean changing words or grammatical forms. Even in modernized texts, Gertrude judges that 'the lady doth [not "does"] protest too much', and Ophelia

---

[25] *The Dramatic Works in the Beaumont and Fletcher Canon*, gen. ed. Fredson Bowers, 10 vols (Cambridge University Press, 1966–1996).

reports that Hamlet 'hath [not "has"] importun'd me with love / In honourable fashion' (Q2 C4^v, 3.2.224; TLN 576–577, 1.3.109–10). Equally, modernization does not mean altering verbal morphology such as what may look to a modern reader like a plural subject with a singular verb—for example, 'The great man down, you mark his favourites flies' (*Hamlet*, F TLN 2072, 3.2.19) or Gonzalo's complaint that 'My old bones aches' (*Tempest*, F TLN 1517, 3.3.2). As Jonathan Hope explains in *Shakespeare's Grammar*, in early modern English there were still 'four possible third person plural endings in the present tense' (-es, -en, -th, and what he calls 'zero'), all of which had been retained from Middle English. He notes (having fun with his own name) that while the 'zero' option ('the men hope') had become the default form by the time of Shakespeare, the other three were still common enough ('the men hopes', 'the men hopen', 'the men hopeth').[26] A modernizing editor is not obliged to change these forms.

In modernizing, it is helpful, not to mention liberating, to realize that the spelling and punctuation in early modern books are not necessarily those of the writer. In the later seventeenth century, Joseph Moxon, in his guide for printers, spells out the compositor's duties. 'A compositor', he argued,

> is strictly to follow his copy . . . but the carelessness of some good authors, and the ignorance of other authors, has forced printers to introduce a custom, which among them is looked upon as a task and duty incumbent on the compositor, viz., to discern and amend the bad spelling and pointing [punctuation] of his copy, if it be English.[27]

Spelling was arguably the province of the compositor not only because, in Moxon's view, the compositor was assumed to have knowledge superior to that of the authors he viewed askance, but also because the compositor

---

[26] Jonathan Hope, *Shakespeare's Grammar* (Bloomsbury Arden Shakespeare, 2003), pp. 161–162.

[27] Joseph Moxon, *Mechanick Exercises, or, The Doctrine of Handy-Works: Applied to the Art of Printing* (1683), ii, pp. 197–198.

exercised control, due to the absence of consistent orthography in the period, over differences between, say, 'shippe' and 'ship' to assist him in 'justifying' his lines, that is, creating, for prose, an even right margin. Differing preferences for spelling certain words – 'do', 'go' and 'here' (or 'doe', 'goe' and 'heere') – have long been held to help distinguish between the work of compositors, although in recent years the value of spelling preferences for identifying compositors has come under question on the premise that they shared the general early modern tendency to be inconsistent in their spelling.[28]

Editors sometimes become attached to certain old-fashioned forms (e.g., 'porpentine' for 'porcupine', 'handkercher' for 'handkerchief', 'murther' for 'murder', and are loath to modernize them, in part believing that they create a period atmosphere appropriate to their text. But keeping such forms leads to a version of English that reflects the language at no particular date. We firmly believe that if you are modernizing you should modernize. By which we mean that if you're going to present the reader with the text of an early modern play in something other than early modern spelling, then you should do so with thoroughness and clarity. There is no workable halfway house. Partial but not full modernization can lead to error, since the eye has to adjust in a random way between old and modern spelling, and given how easy it is to incorporate error the attempt is best avoided. Sometimes a transcription error is staring you in the face but you simply can't see it, most especially when the text you are editing is one you know so well you could recite it blindfolded. And just as you will always make transcription errors, so you will always miss some modernizations. It is inevitable. So it is best to accept that you will do so, and get a second pair of eyes to help you whenever you can. Pride has no place in editing.

In modernizing spelling and deciding which forms exist currently and independently, it is usual to allow the *Oxford English Dictionary* to be the judge. An *OED* head word usually indicates a word in its modern form, but there can still be complications. For example, if you search for 'porpentine' in the *OED* online, what comes up is the entry for 'porcupine', along with

---

[28] See Pervez Rizvi, 'The Use of Spellings for Compositor Attribution in the First Folio', *Papers of the Bibliographical Society of America* 110 (2026): 1–53.

a lengthy listing of the forms the word took in late Middle English and in the 1500s, including 'porpentine'. On the other hand, if you look up 'murther', you will find it is listed as a header but only as meaning 'a murderer, an assassin' and marked 'obsolete'; if you then look up 'murder', you will find that under the usual definition 'murther' is one of the many forms listed. Problems may also arise in modernizing certain words – good examples are 'travail' and 'metal' – whose single early modern spelling could indicate either of two words now differentiated (travel/travail, mettle/metal), forcing you to choose which meaning is primary when both meanings may be present.[29] In our experience there are certain words whose modernizations you are most likely to miss, including 'spight' for 'spite' and 'spright' for 'sprite', the latter a common error because the early modern spelling is retained in the modern word 'sprightly'. The single most common editorial error of modernization, we have found, is a failure to notice when 'then' – as in Hamlet's 'A little more then kin, and lesse then kinde' (TLN 245) – should be modernized to 'than'. An editor becomes very quickly accustomed to early modern spelling, and you need to keep a beady eye on every word that you believe you have modernized.

Another problem of modernization is posed by elisions. These may be present in the early text, either marked – 'Beliu't Ophelia, therefore keepe a loofe' (Q1 *Hamlet* C2^r) or 'Be-monster not thy feature, wer't my fitnes' (Q *King Lear* H4^r) – or unmarked but implied by the metre – 'Even with the vaile and darkning of the sunne' (Q *Troilus and Cressida* L4^r). Whether or not you should spell out final '-ed' endings of past tenses and participles will probably be indicated in your guidelines: for the series we general edit, endings of past tenses and past participles are spelled out even when the early text indicates an unstressed syllable by using an apostrophe. 'O my follies, then Edgar was abus'd' (Q *Lear* H2^r) becomes '... then Edgar was abused'. If the '-ed' is to be stressed, then note this in a CN. Some earlier editions tended to indicate pronunciation by adding an accent – 'When he the ambitious Norway combatèd' (*Hamlet* 1.1.60) – but most current

---

[29] For discussion of homonyms and editing, see the section on 'Word' in Margreta de Grazia and Peter Stallybrass, 'The Materiality of the Shakespearean Text', *Shakespeare Quarterly* 44 (1993): 255–283 (262–266).

editions tend not to: so, for instance, they have 'Of unimproved mettle, hot and full' (1.1.95) for 'Of vnimprooued mettle, hot and full' (Q2 B2ᵛ) and a CN to indicate the stress on the '-ed' in 'unimprovèd'. Whether to spell out polysyllabic adjectives and participles ('med'cine', 'threat'ning') may also be indicated by the guidelines, if you are editing for a series. There may also be indications of when and when not to use apostrophes in verb elisions. Normally, the rule is not to use an apostrophe in modals ('didst', 'shouldst') but to do so with other verbs ('call'st', 'think'st'). In general, these rules apply to verse. In prose, modernization usually calls for spelling out words fully. For certain words you may be able to consult the guidelines or your general editor (do you spell the word 'blessed' or 'blest', 'burned' or 'burnt'?). Otherwise, if you must make the decision yourself, the most important thing is to keep a list and be consistent.

Not surprisingly, modernizing proper nouns can create challenges – both characters' names and place names. In Act 3 of William Rowley's *The Birth of Merlin*, for instance, the Clown is in conversation with Merlin and his father the Devil, and he puns nervously on a number of place names. One is 'Laytonbuzzard', which modernizes straightforwardly enough to 'Leighton Buzzard' and simply needs a CN to explain both that it is a town in Bedfordshire and that a buzzard, a common hawk in England, was considered a particularly stupid bird. Another place named by the Clown, though, is 'Hell-bree', which is more problematic for an editor. In modern spelling, this is 'Hilbre', a small island off the coast of the Wirral Peninsula in north-west England, but the context – the presence of the Devil on stage – means that there is verbal play on Hil/Hell, and if the editor modernizes, the pun becomes invisible. (The solution, we think, is to modernize to 'Hilbre' and to provide both a TN showing the Q spelling '*Hell-bree*' and a CN explaining the pun.)

Personal names can also present challenges for the modernizing editor. Even English names may appear in many spellings: the first two pages of the 1597 quarto of *Richard II* spell Bolingbroke's (or Bullingbrooke's) enemy as 'Mowbray', 'Moubray' and 'Mowbraie' ('Mowbraies charge'); modernizing them is necessary but gives an unjustified sense of textual stability. Or take the character called 'Fluellen' in Shakespeare's *Henry V*. To a Welsh speaker, it is obvious that 'Fluellen' is an attempt at a phonetic rendering of the name Llywelyn [ɬəˈwɛlɪn], which has many variations due to the difficulty for non-Welsh speakers of representing the sound of the initial double *ll* (technically, a voiceless alveolar lateral fricative, which can sound something like 'thl' to non-Welsh-speaking anglophone listeners). Outside Welsh-speaking contexts the name is generally spelled 'Llewellyn', which is often pronounced 'loo-ell-in', without the fricative. The editor of *Henry V* therefore faces a challenge: how fully to modernize the name in a way that respects the Welsh language and archipelagic history while recognizing that the modernization might, for many speakers, produce a sound even less like the Welsh pronunciation of Llywelyn than does Shakespeare's 'Fluellen'.[30] And, in a further complication, in the case of a Shakespearean character (as opposed to a clown in a play by Rowley), there is likely to be a long reception history of spelling and pronouncing the name in a particular way that must be taken into account. Whichever spelling the editor chooses, she will need to provide a commentary note to explain her choice.

Modernizing punctuation is another significant editorial challenge. To reiterate, there is no indication that the punctuation you find in an early modern play text is that of the playwright. Ben Jonson, who actually spent time working on his proofs in the print shop and fussed a good deal about punctuation, is the outlier in this regard. Although actors have sometimes claimed that the punctuation in the First Folio reflects breathing pauses and emphasis *as indicated by Shakespeare*, there is no evidence whatsoever to support this. On the contrary, the one manuscript we have that is probably in Shakespeare's handwriting is the three-page section written by 'Hand D' in the manuscript play *Sir Thomas More*. Lines in this manuscript include almost no punctuation, suggesting that Shakespeare and the other experienced playwrights with whom he was collaborating were well aware that if the play came to be printed, their spelling and rudimentary punctuation would be adjusted by the compositors or by a scribe. We are able to identify the work of the King's Men scribe Ralph Crane, who prepared the manuscripts for at least five plays in the Shakespeare First Folio, by his preference for abundant punctuation, including parentheses, and for 'massed entries', a classical format which called for listing in the opening stage direction all the characters who will appear at

---

[30] See Rory Loughnane and Willy Maley's invaluable discussion in *Editing Archipelagic Shakespeare* (Cambridge University Press, 2024), esp. 33–44.

any point in a scene. Folio plays not copied by Crane do not show these characteristics. That the Folio opens and closes with plays copied by Crane may suggest that the compilers approved or preferred his interventions.[31]

Much of the punctuation in early modern dramatic texts is 'rhetorical', that is, it reflects the rhythm of an imagined speaking voice with a sequence to the implied pauses, with a comma indicating a brief pause, a semi-colon a longer pause, and a colon often present where the twenty-first-century writer would probably put a period (a full stop). In addition, '?' could represent either a question or an exclamation in the early modern period, meaning that the editor must decide which is appropriate for the context. Modern punctuation is, on the other hand, grammatical, dividing up sentences by a structural logic of parts rather than sounds. So, for example, there are different rules for commas depending on whether a group of words is a phrase, a dependent modifier or a clause. In general, current usage calls for a light hand whereas in a nineteenth-century edition of Shakespeare, for instance, sentences would typically be broken into many parts.

A few examples may help clarify the issues an editor faces.

> *Cam.* *Sicilia* cannot shew himselfe ouer-kind to *Bohemia*: They were trayn'd together in their Child-hoods; and there rooted betwixt them then such an affection, which cannot chuse but braunch now. Since their more mature Dignities,and Royall Necessities(made seperation of their Societie, their Encounters(though not Personall) hath been Royally attornyed with enter-change of Gifts,Letters,louing Embassies,that they haue seem'd to be together,though absent:shooke hands,as ouer a Vast; and embrac'd as it were from the ends of oppofed Winds. The Heauens continue their Loues.

Figure 10 William Shakespeare, F *Winter's Tale* TLN 24-34 – RBD EL SH15M 1623, reproduced by kind permission of the Free Library of Philadelphia, Rare Book Department

---

[31] For discussion of Crane and *Cymbeline*, see Valerie Wayne, ed., *Cymbeline*, *The Arden Shakespeare Third Series* (Bloomsbury Publishing, 2017), pp. 384–389.

Figure 10 is a prose speech (TLN 24–34) from the opening of *The Winter's Tale* (a Folio-only play) from which a modern editor would probably remove many of the commas. A modernized version of this speech might look like the following, with fewer commas and without the scribe Crane's characteristic round brackets:

> Sicilia cannot show himself over-kind to Bohemia. They were trained together in their childhoods, and there rooted betwixt them then such an affection which cannot choose but branch now. Since their more mature dignities and royal necessities made separation of their society, their encounters, though not personal, hath been royally attorneyed with interchange of gifts, letters, loving embassies, that they have seemed to be together, though absent; shook hands as over a vast; and embraced as it were from the ends of opposed winds.

Again, Figure 11 shows a verse speech by Richard II (TLN 1505–14). In this text, from a play entirely in verse, the Folio punctuation could be seen to direct the actor, with, for example, a meaningful pause after 'wills' and perhaps a change of tone after 'And yet not so'.

> Let's talke of Graues, of Wormes, and Epitaphs,
> Make Dust our Paper, and with Raynie eyes
> Write Sorrow on the Bosome of the Earth.
> Let's chuse Executors, and talke of Wills:
> And yet not so; for what can we bequeath,
> Saue our deposed bodies to the ground?
> Our Lands, our Liues, and all are *Bullingbrookes*,
> And nothing can we call our owne, but Death,
> And that small Modell of the barren Earth,
> Which serues as Paste, and Couer to our Bones:

Figure 11 William Shakespeare, F *Richard II* TLN 1505-14 – RBD EL SH15M 1623, reproduced by kind permission of the Free Library of Philadelphia, Rare Book Department

Yet a recent editor, following modern practice in keeping punctuation to a minimum, presents the passage like this:

> Let's talk of graves, of worms and epitaphs,
> Make dust our paper and with rainy eyes
> Write sorrow on the bosom of the earth.
> Let's choose executors and talk of wills.
> And yet not so, for what can we bequeath
> Save our deposèd bodies to the ground?
> Our lands, our lives and all are Bolingbroke's,
> And nothing can we call our own but death
> And that small model of the barren earth
> Which serves as paste and cover to our bones.[32]

Notice, too, that the modernizing process also removes all the capitals, whether or not they could be viewed as emphatic.

When you've done your own modern punctuation, then go back and compare your choices with your base text. It may be that the compositor, the most likely source of the punctuation, knew what he was doing; it may be, however, that he was negotiating the effects of a less-than-perfect casting-off process, in which case the use of space will probably be of more importance to him than sense, and he may add or remove punctuation marks accordingly. Equally, there are a few playwrights who over four hundred years have sustained an ability to impose their will on their editors. Ben Jonson is the most obvious example. Have respect for Jonson, but do not be dictated to by him.[33] As with spelling, so with punctuation: if you are going to modernize, modernize.

A caveat, however. The word 'modernization' appears to imply a straightforward binary – early modern spelling and punctuation versus

---

[32] Andrew Gurr, ed., *Richard II*, The New Cambridge Shakespeare, rev. ed. (Cambridge University Press, 2003), pp. 3.2.145–154.

[33] For Jonson's activity as 'editor and reviser of his own texts', see *The Cambridge Edition of the Works of Ben Jonson*, eds. David Bevington, Martin Butler and Ian Donaldson (Cambridge University Press, 2012), 1: lx-lxxxvi (lxviii).

modern spelling and punctuation. But differences between early modern and contemporary usages are not so clear cut. There are, for instance, marked differences between North American and British practice not only in the spelling but also in the punctuation of English. The differences in spelling practice tend to be straightforward, but adapting to the less immediately visible differences in *punctuation* habits can be a challenge (as we wrote this sentence, for instance, we debated the comma before the 'but'). This is especially the case for editors whose first language is not English or who have been educated elsewhere in the world than in anglophone contexts on either side of the Atlantic. If you are a modernizing editor editing for a series published somewhere other than the country in which you were educated, then you will need to adapt your practice to that of the series for which you are editing.

2.6 Emendation

When do you emend your text? That is, when do you depart from the words or punctuation of your base text? This is a different question from modernization, but there are inevitable overlaps or confusions. When, then, is a modernization a modernization, and when is it an emendation? For the majority of texts, as a modernizing editor you are going to do a lot of modernizing and relatively little emending. So, in brief, turning 'porpentine' into 'porcupine' in your edition of *Hamlet* is modernizing, whereas (assuming you have chosen F as your base text) turning 'Politician' into 'pelican' is emending. For an editor of a play with only one early witness – a quarto of a Dekker play, say – emendation is something to be done only when confronted with obvious error. In the same way, if the only text of *Hamlet* that survived were the Folio, then editors, lacking the Quarto reading 'pelican' to inform their decision making, would still in all probability have puzzled over the word 'Politician', tested out ways in which the reading could make sense before deciding that, on the balance of probabilities, the reference is to the myth of the self-sacrificial pelican and emending accordingly, providing a CN to defend the decision. Of course, for the *Hamlet* editor, the existence of three markedly different early texts of the play still means that choices must be made. We will return to this.

Most of the time it is clear enough when an emendation is needed. GM, editing *Henry VIII* for Arden, encountered his first emendation in the first

> *Buck.* An vntimely Ague
> Staid me a Prisoner in my Chamber, when
> Those Sunnes of Glory, those two Lights of Men
> Met in the vale of Andren.
> *Nor.* 'Twixt Guynes and Arde,
> I was then present, saw them salute on Horsebacke,

Figure 12 William Shakespeare and John Fletcher, F *Henry VIII* TLN 44–49 – RBD EL SH15M 1623, reproduced by kind permission of the Free Library of Philadelphia, Rare Book Department

scene (TLN 44–49; see Figure 12). In this opening scene, Buckingham, who missed the meeting of Henry VIII and François I at the Field of the Cloth of Gold because he was ill (or so he claims), encounters Norfolk and asks what happened, mentioning that he knows the two kings met in 'the vale of Andren'. Norfolk offers a slightly more specific location for the meeting: 'Twixt Guynes and Arde'. The latter two locations are clear enough – Guînes and Ardres, villages in the Pas de Calais – and editors have modernized accordingly. 'Andren', though, was emended in the Second Folio of 1632 to 'Arde'; apparently someone in the print shop decided there was no such place as 'Andren' and that Norfolk is naming the village that Buckingham has already mentioned, Ardres. Editors from Rowe onwards have thus emended 'Andren' to 'Ardres'. However, contemporary editors will consult external sources – maps, chronicle histories, and so on – whenever possible. In this case GM, driving through the Pas de Calais, noted that between Guînes and Ardres is another village called Andres and thus that the First Folio reading has locational validity and should arguably not be emended, with Rowe, to 'Ardres'. Instead, he adopted his own emendation: 'Andres' for 'Andren'.

This is a fairly marginal example – not remotely in the league of perhaps the most famous Shakespearean emendation of all. When in 2.3 of *Henry V* the Hostess tells Pistol, Nim and the rest that she is sure Falstaff is dying, she says: 'for after I saw him fumble with the sheets and play with flowers and smile upon his fingers' end, I knew there was but one way: for his nose was as

Editing an Early Modern Play 45

> ......, a parted cu n int betweene 1 weiue and One, eu'n
> at the turning o'th'Tyde: for after I faw him fumble with
> the Sheets, and play with Flowers, and fmile vpon his fingers end, I knew there was but one way: for his Nofe was
> as fharpe as a Pen, and a Table of greene fields. How now
> Sir *Iohn* (quoth I?) what man? be a good cheare : fo a
> cryed out God God God three or foure times

Figure 13 William Shakespeare, F *Henry V* TLN 836–840 – RBD EL SH15M 1623, reproduced by kind permission of the Free Library of Philadelphia, Rare Book Department

sharp as a pen, and 'a babbled of green fields'.[34] Except that in the Folio text (TLN 836–839), the last words of this sentence are 'a Table of greene fields', which is, to say the least, difficult to make sense of (see Figure 13). It was the editor Lewis Theobald, in the eighteenth century, who proposed 'a [i.e. he] babbled' for 'a Table', suggesting both that the compositor had misread a looped form of secretary hand 't' for a 'b' and inferring that Falstaff was reciting Psalm 23: 'The Lord is my shepherd, I shall not want. He maketh me to rest in green pasture, and leadeth me by the still waters', in the words of the Geneva Bible. Subsequent editors have for the most part adopted Theobald's reading as a convincing solution to the crux. Still, not everyone has been happy with the emendation, and some have made ingenious arguments for retaining 'a Table' (Pope, for instance, suggested that the item of furniture in question belonged to a member of the company called Greenfield). Whether or not they are right, there is a nagging sense that babbling of green fields, understood as reciting Psalm 23, is a little too convenient a reading in the context of eighteenth-century Christian sentimentalism, hinting as it does at a deathbed conversion to confound Bardolph's uncertainty about Falstaff's destination, 'either in heaven or in hell'.[35]

But cruxes of this stature, and their emendations, are few and far between. For the most part you will find you emend rarely. Far more

---

[34] Andrew Gurr, ed., *Henry V*, The New Cambridge Shakespeare, rev. ed. (Cambridge University Press, 2005), 2.3.11–14.

[35] For full discussion of the crux, see Gary Taylor, ed., *Henry V* (Oxford University Press, 1982), pp. 192–195.

often, and equally controversially, you will be rejecting an eighteenth- or nineteenth-century editor's familiar emendation that you consider unnecessary, or you will be agreeing with a previous editor that a stage direction needs to be inserted to clarify action, or you will be dealing with a problem of lineation (which we address in the next section), or you will be modernizing punctuation in a way that you realize might affect the meaning of the line and that therefore needs serious thought. In other words, your editorial activities will be many and varied, but you will find that you emend little in comparison with the other requirements of editing.

This said, if (as is, we assume, unlikely if you are a first-time editor) your play exists in more than one early authoritative text – in other words, if there is more than one possible base text – then you have a more complex task, since you will have options for emendation not necessarily of cruxes but of readings that you would not register as material for emendation were it not for the alternative reading offered in the other extant text. Probably the best-known instance of this in the Shakespeare canon is the difference between the variants at a key moment in Q and F *Othello*. Just before he kills himself, Othello compares himself to a racial other who did not realize the unparalleled value of what he had until it was too late. The wording in Q (N2^r) is noticeably different from that in F (TLN 3657–3659): see Figures 14 and 15.[36] Each reading makes sense, so how is an editor to choose between the options: 'Indian' or 'Iudean'? Are these two different

> Perplext in the extreame ; of one whose hand,
> Like the base *Indian*, threw a pearle away,
> Richer then all his Tribe : of one whose subdued eyes,

Figure 14 William Shakespeare, Q1 *Othello* N2^r – STC 22305 copy 1, reproduced by kind permission of the Folger Shakespeare Library

---

[36] See Scott McMillin, ed., The First Quarto of Othello, ' The New Cambridge Shakespeare: The Early Quartos' (Cambridge University Press, 2001), 5.2.362–64.

> Perplexed in the extreame: Of one, whose hand
> (Like the base Iudean) threw a Pearle away
> Richer then all his Tribe: Of one, whose subdu'd Eyes,

Figure 15 William Shakespeare, F *Othello* TLN 3657-3659 – RBD EL SH15M 1623, reproduced by kind permission of the Free Library of Philadelphia, Rare Book Department

intended readings, or is one or the other a typesetting error? The possible errors are clear enough: misreading of secretary hand 'i' and 'e' (which could be near-indistinguishable, especially if the tittle – the dot over 'i' – is mixed up with punctuation straying down from the line above) and/or of secretary hand 'n' and 'u' (which can also be difficult to distinguish). There is also the possibility, as in the *All's Well* and *Philaster* passages we cited earlier, of a 'turned letter' or 'foul case' (there are in fact several instances of turned 'u' and 'n' in Folio *Othello*). Both these possibilities for error could work either way, however, supporting either reading, and in the end there is no proven basis for a decision other than the editor's own preference. Yet the editorial choice between the words 'Indian' and 'Judean' (or 'Judaean' as it would normally be modernized) cannot exactly be an unburdened one, given the cultural function of racial stereotypes not only in 1622 and 1623 (the dates, respectively, of Q and F) but also four hundred years later. Both options are, after all, based in racist assumptions – 'Judean' referencing Judas Iscariot ('Judaean' where the other disciples were 'Galilean'), thereby tapping into the prevalence of antisemitic sentiment in Calvinist early modern England, while 'Indian' signifies the alleged ignorance of the people of India (according to classical sources including Pliny) of the true value of the precious stones found in their mines but also, very probably, disparages the native Americans being displaced and killed at this time by English colonists in Virginia. A twenty-first-century editor, discussing this crux, has a responsibility to address the textual, historical and cultural contexts together if she is to account for the implications of the choice she makes in editing the text.

Current editorial practice, as it happens, offers options that simplify editorial choices at such moments. One such practice is that of 'unediting', an approach that offers a radical critique of processes of emendation and modernization, arguing that any resolution of a crux may suppress meaning latent in the text and that the text is hence best presented to the reader with minimal editorial intervention, or indeed none. Another is 'single-text editing', the mode we chose as general textual editors for *The Norton Shakespeare, Third Edition*. Adopting this methodology means you are editing a *text*, not the *play*, and you will produce an edition that is not the result of your own picking and choosing from pairs of options but, rather, one that follows your base text unless a particular reading is manifestly untenable. This method usually removes the need for a decision; you will simply provide a TN noting the reading in the other early text and perhaps a CN to discuss it. This sounds straightforward, and it stops you for the most part from exercising critical judgement about the rival options. But if, like us, you grew up reading conflated editions of multi-text Shakespeare plays, including of *Othello*, then you will find that, if you are editing a play from the Shakespeare canon for which there is more than one feasible base text, you will at times be obliged to retain a reading that is not the one you prefer but that is the reading in the base text you have chosen. It also does not eliminate the need to recognize error.[37] Such is life and editing in the second quarter of the twenty-first century. It will, as editing methodologies always do, change.

We will conclude this section by doffing our caps to a major editor of Shakespeare and directing you to Stanley Wells's *Re-editing Shakespeare for the Modern Reader*, in which he discusses the modernization of spelling and anatomizes a series of emendations, and their implications, in a range of plays in the Shakespeare canon.[38] Note, though, that, as so often, there is no equivalent essay for plays by playwrights other than Shakespeare. It is,

---

[37] See John Jowett, 'Shakespeare and the Kingdom of Error', in *The New Oxford Shakespeare: Critical Reference Edition*, eds. Gary Taylor, John Jowett, Terri Bourus and Gabriel Egan (Oxford University Press, 2017), pp. 1: xlix–lxiv.

[38] Stanley Wells, *Re-editing Shakespeare for the Modern Reader* (Oxford University Press, 1984).

much of the time, the task of the editor of plays by all other early modern playwrights to extrapolate, adjust and reinvent processes designed first and foremost for the Shakespeare canon.

2.7 Lineation

Lineation is the formal term for the way in which the lines of a text are divided and arranged on the page. Negotiating the lineation in an early printed text can be a challenge. The words as they are set out on the printed page from time to time conflict with the rhythm of the lines – this can happen for a range of reasons including, for instance, a casting off process that has gone awry – and one of the editor's tasks is to listen for the metre and to try to set out the words in metrically appropriate groupings. Some playwrights played fast and loose with the verse more than others, or like Shakespeare became more metrically free with time (a good reason to read through your author's works chronologically, if possible). It is noticeable, for instance, that there are significantly more lineation challenges in the scenes of *The Changeling* normally attributed to Middleton than in those considered Rowley's, even as Rowley seems as a general rule to have been less of a stickler for the strict pentameter. Classically trained editors in the eighteenth and nineteenth centuries often had good ears for metre and turned dense pages of apparent prose or of over-long verse lines into consistent pentameters. But they also at times overdid it, forcing metre onto prose or being overly rigid with metrical consistency at the expense of what might be viewed as appropriate writerly flexibility (or roughness) in the verse. The first editors of *The Changeling* in the nineteenth century, Charles Dilke and Alexander Dyce, worked hard to impose consistent versification throughout the play; the question for the twenty-first-century editor is whether or not to see this as appropriate.

Keep an eye on your working premises for lineation. Beware, for instance, of the assumption that characters of higher rank must always speak in verse. In *Henry IV, Part I*, both Hotspur and Prince Henry use verse *and* prose; in *Twelfth Night*, the conversation between Sebastian and the pirate Antonio is in prose in 2.1 and in verse in 3.3; and the speeches of Prince Hal's braggart companion Pistol are a mixture of verse and prose.

> *Enter Ghost, and Hamlet.*
> Ham. Whether wilt thou leade me, speake, Ile goe no further.
> Ghoſt. Marke me.
> Ham. I will.
> Ghoſt. My houre is almoſt come
> When I to ſulphrus and tormenting flames
> Muſt render vp my ſelfe.
> Ham. Alas poore Ghoſt.

Figure 16 William Shakespeare, Q2 *Hamlet* D2^r – STC 22276, reproduced by kind permission of the Folger Shakespeare Library

Playwrights, not least Shakespeare, were so accustomed to thinking in pentameters that the reader can find impeccably metrical sentences in the midst of prose. The opening lines of 1.5 of *Hamlet* in the 1604 second quarto (D2^r) are presented as seven separate lines (see Figure 16). Modern editors usually reduce these to four, with the first as prose and the second a pentameter in three parts:

Hamlet	Whither wilt thou lead me? Speak. I'll go no further.
Ghost	Mark me.
Hamlet	I will.
Ghost	My hour is almost come
	When I to sulphurous and tormenting flames
	Must rend up myself.
Hamlet	Alas, poor ghost.[39]

An editor will do so because it is reasonable to assume, in a verse scene, that shared or half lines will, when assembled, add up to consistent pentameters. But because Shakespeare seemed to breathe in iambic pentameters, there are numerous places where it is simply up to the editor to determine whether a line is to be treated as prose or verse. For the Folio-only plays, it also sometimes seems that the narrow

---

[39] Philip Edwards, ed.; Heather Hirschfeld, rev., *Hamlet*, The New Cambridge Shakespeare (Cambridge University Press, 2019), 1.5.1–4.

double columns may have made the compositor adjust the lineation to fit – an instance being the first scene of *Antony and Cleopatra*, where the Folio prints as the fourth and fifth lines, 'Haue glow'd like plated Mars: / Now bend, now turne' (TLN 4–7), even though the pentameter is regular. In *The Changeling* 1.2 (Q B4v), Alibius and Lollio are talking about the former's wife, Isabella (see Figure 17). As befits their respective statuses, Alibius speaks in verse, Lollio in prose, but Alibius's verse lines are less than elegant, and Lollio, although he speaks otherwise in consistent prose, at one point produces a more regular pentameter line – 'So much the worse to be kept secret, sir' – than any his master speaks. The editor must be sensitive to these issues, setting out such lines as verse on the page where it seems logical to do so but not necessarily marking what might be viewed as an 'accidental' pentameter as verse. At such moments, as is often the case in editing, the editor has to deal with challenging issues of authorial **intention**: Did the writer intend this line to be metrically exact? In how many ways is this an impossible question to answer? Does the *Changeling* editor give Lollio one line of verse among the prose? Or does she decide that this line of apparent verse is the result of Rowley's tendency to produce pentameters even when he doesn't mean to?

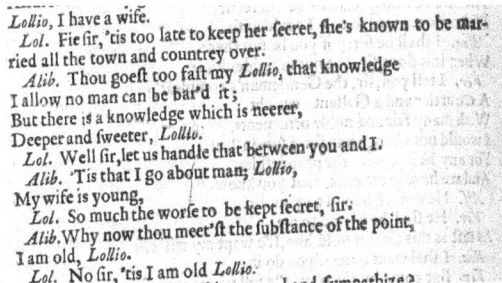

Figure 17 Thomas Middleton and William Rowley, Q *Changeling* B4^v – M1980, reproduced by kind permission of the Folger Shakespeare Library

It is not only prose and verse distinctions that are up to the editor. If you turn back to the passage from Q *King Lear* that we cited earlier ('Let him fly far'), you will see that Gloucester's speech begins with a half line. In the quarto, the preceding speech (by Edmund, or 'the bastard' as he is called in the quarto), ends as follows:

> . . . when he saw my best alarumd spirits,
> bould in the quarrels, right, rousd to the encounter, or whether
> gasted by the noyse I made, but sodainly he fled. (D4ʳ)

Editors tend to turn Edmund's entire speech into verse, concluding, 'But suddenly he fled', so they can complete the line with the first four words of Gloucester's speech:

> But suddenly he fled.
> *Gloucester*   Let him fly far.

Staircasing, or aligning the beginning of the second half of the line with the end of the first half, is a convention not usually found in the early texts, and while it is standard in modernized editions, it frequently leaves an editor with difficult choices. In *Macbeth* (for which we have only the Folio text), Macduff reports the death of Duncan (TLN 820–825):

> Most sacrilegious Murther hath broke ope
> The Lords anoynted Temple, and stole thence
> The Life o'th' Building.
>   *Macb.* What Is't you say, the Life?
>   *Lenox.* Meane you his Maiestie?

Here there are three half- or part lines: 'The Life o'th' Building'; 'What Is't you say, the Life?'; and 'Meane you his Maiestie?'. How might an editor address the conflicting possibilities? Some reduce this passage to four lines on the basis that 'The Life o'th' Building' and 'What Is't you say, the Life?' together form a workable pentameter:

>   Most sacrilegious murder hath broke ope
>   The Lord's anointed temple, and stole thence,
>   The life o'th' building.
>
> *Macbeth*   What is't you say? The life?
> *Lennox*   Mean you his majesty?

Others, not convinced, retain the Folio lineation.[40] In both cases, Lennox's 'Mean you his majesty?' remains incomplete, metrically speaking. The editor must choose, but there may be moments when she is less than wholly convinced by the choice she makes.

Editors of early modern plays need to develop an ear for verse. It helps enormously to be able to, or to learn to, 'hear' a pentameter. Rearranging lines into workable metre is invaluable for helping you guide readers in hearing the lines in their own heads. You will wish to add CNs on unexpected stresses when a polysyllabic word such as 'companion' is to be pronounced with four syllables rather than three in order for the metre to work: 99 per cent of your readers will need help at such moments. You will also need to become familiar with the method for recording lineation changes used by the particular series or edition for which you are working. At times, oddly enough, your choice of verse or prose will not necessarily be visible to the reader simply because of the rules of the series: in Arden Early Modern Drama editions, for instance, a line of verse starts below the speech prefix, while prose follows the prefix on the same line; this, by contrast, is not the rule for, say, the New Cambridge Shakespeare series.

2.8 Textual Notes

We gave a brief definition of **textual notes** earlier, and it is now time to look more closely at what a textual note is and how it is formulated – not least because TNs are largely incomprehensible to readers when they first encounter them. (The textual scholar Thomas Berger memorably referred to the TNs at the bottom of the page of an edition as the 'band of terror'.) It

---

[40] See, for instance, A. R. Braunmuller, ed., *Macbeth*, *The New Cambridge Shakespeare* (Cambridge University Press, 1997), 2.3.60–64.

is worth noting, however, that in editions designed primarily for teaching (such as *The Norton Shakespeare*), textual notes are usually simplified, seldom recording changes to lineation or punctuation and sometimes, rather than identifying individual editors, merely using the abbreviation '*Edd*' to indicate that an emendation comes from somewhere in the editorial tradition. Also, since the landmark 1986 *Oxford Shakespeare* was published with a separate 'Textual Companion', there has been a growing trend to publish textual notes separately, sometimes (only) in a digital format. Both of these moves are understandable, given that textual notes are usually of interest only to other editors and textual scholars. Nonetheless, it seems to us less than ideal either to reduce still further the information compressed into a TN or to relegate it to a separate volume or to a website unlikely to be accessed by many, since to do so makes invisible much of the work the editor has done to create an accessible and informative reading experience. For our purposes in this Element, we will describe the kind of TN you will find in a single-volume scholarly critical edition.

There are basically two types of textual notes: those that record emendations of words and those that record other editorial changes such as the insertion of stage directions or missing speech prefixes. Both have the same purpose: to allow the reader to reconstruct, in her mind's eye, the base text from which the edition has been created. Here are two instances from GM's Arden Shakespeare Third Series edition of Shakespeare and Fletcher's *Henry VIII*:[41]

> [74 SD] *Theobald*
> [34 *out*] *Collier*^{4}; wee *F*; weare *F2*

Textual notes such as these may be offputtingly cryptic. In tacit acknowledgement, they are usually situated at the bottom of the page of a critical edition, or printed in a smaller font, and they may not even be noticed by many readers. Yet if you can parse them, they contain valuable information about the choices the editor has made and about the nature of her interventions in the text.

---

[41] Gordon McMullan, ed., *King Henry VIII*, 'The Arden Shakespeare Third Series' (Bloomsbury Publishing, 2004), pp. 284, 253.

There is specific terminology for the elements of a textual note. For the first of the *Henry VIII* examples, they are as follows: line reference ('74'); lemma (an ancient Greek word for the headword of a gloss, that is, the reading or editorial interpolation quoted from the present edition, in this case 'SD', meaning a stage direction inserted by the editor); and siglum (a Latin word, a diminutive, meaning the abbreviated form used for the source of the lemma, in this case the editor who first added the stage direction, the eighteenth-century editor Lewis Theobald). The second example similarly begins with the line reference ('34'), lemma ('*oui*') and siglum ('*Collier*[4]') and then includes the form in which the lemma appears in the base text ('wee', followed by the siglum for the base text, '*F*', that is, the First Folio) and then a further reading ('weare'), which is that of the Second Folio ('*F2*').

What do these textual notes tell the reader?

The first example is for 2.2.74 (TLN 1118): 'Thou art a cure fit for a king. [*to Campeius*] You're welcome' (see Figure 18 for the Folio text without a SD). The TN here means that an editorial stage direction, one first created by Theobald in his edition of 1733 (and hence placed in square brackets in the text as an editorial interpolation), has been adopted in GM's edition to make the stage action clearer for the reader. The king is speaking to two cardinals, and he switches address from one to the other midline; Theobald and subsequent editors add the SD to make sure the reader understands that the king shifts his focus to Cardinal Campeius during the line. To an audience member this will be obvious – the king will turn to address Campeius – but it may not be so clear to a reader.

> *Enter Wolfey and Campeius with a Commiffion.*
> Who's there? my good Lord Cardinall? O my *Wolfey*,
> The quiet of my wounded Confcience;
> Thou art a cure fit for a King; you'r welcome
> Moft learned Reuerend Sir, into our Kingdome,
> Vfe vs, and it: My good Lord, haue great care,
> I be not found a Talker.

Figure 18 William Shakespeare and John Fletcher, F *Henry VIII* TLN 1115-1121 – RBD EL SH15M 1623, reproduced by kind permission of the Free Library of Philadelphia, Rare Book Department

> Or pack to their old Playfellowes;there, I take it,
> They may *Cum Priuilegio*, wee away
> The lag end of their lewdneſſe, and be laugh'd at.

Figure 19 William Shakespeare and John Fletcher, F *Henry VIII* TLN 611-613 – reproduced by kind permission of the Free Library of Philadelphia, Rare Book Department

The second is for 1.3.34 (TLN 612): 'They may, *cum privilegio, oui* away' (see Figure 19). The TN explains an editorial decision, one first made by the editor John Payne Collier in his fourth edition of the plays of Shakespeare in 1878, to modernize the First Folio's 'wee' to '*oui*' (the context is an English courtier poking fun at his French counterparts). The TN also tells the reader that whoever edited the Shakespeare Second Folio of 1632 'corrected' the First Folio's 'wee' (for French '*oui*') to 'weare', but that editors since Theobald have decided that this 'correction' was in fact an error. This TN is accompanied by a commentary note explaining that the First Folio's 'wee' plays on the sense of urination, which may be lost to the reader, if not necessarily to an audience member hearing the line, with the modernization to '*oui*'. (The editor also needs to gloss '*cum privilegio*', which is short for '*cum privilegio ad imprimendum solum*', meaning 'the sole right to print', a formula noting a printer's monopoly of the publication of a particular text.)

The logic of textual notes of this kind is to present, as briefly as possible, information about choices the editor has made in respect of issues arising from the base text without using a word count that would, across the length of the edition, be prohibitive. Similarly, the sigla, abbreviations such as '*Collier*[4]', refer to a list of references included in the edition that provides full bibliographical details (heavily compressed as such references necessarily are in TNs). Most of the time, the textual note is enough to explain the decision that has been made, but sometimes a commentary note is needed in addition – as with 'wee'/'*oui*' and the implication of urination – in order to explain wordplay that might be hidden, in this case by the process of modernization. The extent of textual notes will vary very much by edition, once again implicitly determined by the perceived needs of the anticipated reader. In a two-text play such as *Othello*, for which there is both the Folio text and an early Quarto, TNs will typically report differences between them. A simple TN – 'my *F*; our *Q*' – records a significant difference between the two texts as Desdemona requests either that Emilia lay out '*my* wedding sheets' (F TLN 2807) or '*our* wedding sheets' (Q K4^v).[42] Textual notes may also record, among other things, altered lineation and its source (i.e., the editor who first emended the lineation), modernizations of words or punctuation that affect meaning or metrics, and (as we have noted) added or moved stage directions.

Added stage directions offer a clear instance of the fine line an editor treads when amplifying the base text for increased readerly comprehension. Such SDs function to make what will normally be obvious to an audience member observing a performance apparent also to a reader looking only at the printed page – a process that requires a great deal of sensitivity, especially if your edition's potential readership includes theatre professionals. If your play has been edited previously, various stage directions will no doubt have been added by an earlier editor; these always need reviewing to ensure that they provide necessary information and are not, say, the conviction of a particular editor that a certain action must happen at a certain moment. Editors, though they might at times convince themselves otherwise, are not always capable directors – and they must also remain aware of the indeterminacies of early modern staging.[43] Sometimes, too, cultural changes can require adjustment to the phrasing of a stage direction. In 2.2 of *The Changeling*, for instance, Beatrice-Joanna and Alsemero meet. See Figure 20 for their exchange in Q (D1^v). Modern editors add '[*Kisses her.*]' after 'equals', picking up on Beatrice-Joanna's 'This poor kiss'. This seems reasonable enough. A twenty-first-century editor, though, may wish

---

[42] Norman Sanders, ed.; Christina Luckyj, rev., *Othello, The New Cambridge Shakespeare* (Cambridge University Press, 2018), 4.2.111.

[43] On editorial stage directions and questions of early modern staging, see Margaret Jane Kidnie, 'Text, Performance, and the Editors: Staging Shakespeare's Drama', *Shakespeare Quarterly* 51 (2000): 456-73.

> *Alf.* W'are so like in our expreſſions, Lady, that unleſs I borrow
> The ſame words, I ſhall never find their equals.
>   *Bea.* How happy were this meeting, this embrace,
> If it were free from envy? This poor kiſs
> It has an enemy, a hatefull one,
> That wiſhes poyſon to't : how well were I now
> If there were none ſuch name known as *Piracquo* ?

Figure 20 Thomas Middleton and William Rowley, Q *Changeling* D1ᵛ –
M1980, reproduced by kind permission of the Folger Shakespeare Library

to reflect on the gendered agency implied in this added SD – especially given the play's insistent representation of sexual coercion – and replace it with '[*They kiss*.]' to make clear to the reader that this is to be understood as a rare moment of mutuality in the play.

Added SDs require awareness not only of cultural change of this kind but, above all, of theatrical practicalities – the practicalities, that is, both of the early modern stage (in the case of *The Changeling*, the indoor Cockpit/ Phoenix playhouse) and of the possibilities for modern staging. One change that is frequently needed is the moving of an entry direction so that the character entering is already visible to those on the stage by the time they acknowledge in the dialogue the new character's arrival. The TN may reveal that an editor has had to do this regularly, whether because the entries were ambiguously placed in the underlying manuscript (e.g., in the margin) or because the manuscript was a composite, containing materials from multiple documents, possibly including a promptbook.

Entry directions in *The Changeling* frequently need to be moved, usually by just one line. During the first, lengthy scene of the play, for instance, two sets of characters, Beatrice-Joanna and Alsemero and their subordinates Diaphanta and Jasperino, speak 'apart' – that is, they stand sufficiently far apart on the stage for the audience to accept that one pair's dialogue cannot be heard by the other pair (B3ʳ) (see Figure 21). During Jasperino's flirtatious conversation with Diaphanta, Beatrice-Joanna's father Vermandero enters, and she quickly warns Alsemero, who has yet to meet Vermandero, that he has arrived: 'My father, sir', she says, arguably

> *Bea.* I am no enemy to any creature
> My memory has, but yon' Gentleman.
> *Alf.* He does ill to tempt your sight, if he knew it.
> *Bea.* He cannot be ignorant of that Sir,
> I have not spar'd to tell him so, and I want
> To help my self, since he's a Gentleman
> In good respect with my father, and follows him.
> *Alf.* He's out of his place then now.
> *Jaf.* I am a mad Wag, wench.
> *Dia.* So me thinks; but for your comfort I can tell you, we have a Doctor in the Citie that undertakes the cure of such.
> *Jaf.* Tush, I know what Physick is best for the state of mine own body.
> *Dia.* 'Tis scarce a well govern'd state, I beleeve.
> *Jaf.* I could shew thee such a thing with an Ingredian that we two would compound together, and if it did not tame the maddest blood i'th town for two hours after, Ile nere profess Physick agen.
> *Dia.* A little poppy Sir, were good to cause you sleep.
> *Jaf.* Poppy: I'le give thee a pop i'th lips for that first, and begin there: Poppy is one simple indeed, and Cuckow (what you call't) another: I'le discover no more now, another time I'le shew thee all.
> *Bea.* My Father, Sir.   *Enter Vermandero and Servants.*
> *Ver.* Oh *Joanna*, I came to meet thee, your devotion's ended.

Figure 21 Thomas Middleton and William Rowley, Q *Changeling* B3ʳ – M1980, reproduced by kind permission of the Folger Shakespeare Library

(though not necessarily) as an aside. Q places '*Enter Vermandero and Servants*' immediately after she says this, but since she cannot have seen her father if he has not yet entered, it seems necessary for an editor to adjust the order slightly, as here:

JASPERINO Poppy? I'll give thee a pop i'th' lips for that first and begin there. Poppy is one simple indeed, and cuckoo what-you-call't another. I'll discover no more now; another time I'll show thee all.

Enter VERMANDERO *and* SERVANTS.

BEATRICE-JOANNA [*to Alsemero*]
    My father, sir.
VERMANDERO O Joanna, I came to meet thee.
Your devotion's ended?

In performance, a director may arrange the action so that Beatrice-Joanna sees her father through a doorway before he has technically entered the stage, meaning that the SD could in theory stay where Q places it, but the editor's responsibility to the reader means she probably needs to move it a line earlier. This may seem trivial, but it is the kind of decision that editors of early modern plays must make all the time, and it requires a TN to show the reader that the change has been made. In this case, since Douglas Bruster seems to have been the first editor to move this SD, the TN would be: 154 SD] *Bruster; after* sir *Q*.[44]

Note that in a TN you only cite the first editor to make a change and, except in the rarest of cases, you are not obliged to record alternative possibilities that you reject. (Do not, in other words, use textual notes for the purpose of critical warfare. Only record other options you have not selected if you think they have sufficient validity that the reader will benefit from knowing about them or from seeing the history of an emendation. Some series instruct editors only to record rejected readings in a TN if the editor mentions them in a CN.) Similarly, accept that you are highly unlikely to establish an entirely new reading, at least if you are editing a play in the Shakespeare canon or a frequently edited play such as, say, Webster's *The Duchess of Malfi* or Ford's *'Tis Pity She's a Whore*. In these cases, you are much more likely to build on the work of previous editors than to create an entirely new reading. But sometimes you do, and if so, the siglum is '*this edn*'. If you are editing a play that has rarely been edited, you are far more likely to find that you wish to make a new emendation or, say, move an entry direction that nobody has previously moved. Nonetheless, beware: the urge to include a '*this edn*' in your edition can be a distraction. As so often in the task of editing, your ego should be left at home. If you do find you can make a new emendation – a genuine '*this edn*' – then congratulations, but an edition of a play will be none the worse if you find no such possibility. GM's emendation in the first scene of his Arden Third Series *Henry VIII* – emending F's 'Andren ... Guynes ... Arde' to

---

[44] Douglas Bruster, ed., *The Changeling*, in *Thomas Middleton: The Collected Works*, eds. Gary Taylor and John Lavagnino (Oxford University Press, 2007), pp. 1632–1678 (1640).

'Andres ... Guînes ... Ardres' – gave him his one and only '*this edn*', and very proud he was too, though you could argue that this wasn't exactly emendation – it was more akin to regularization and modernization of the slightly confused place names in F. In any case, imagine his consternation when it dawned on him that this immortal editorial moment would for evermore bear as its siglum not '*McMullan*' but '*Ard*^{3}'.

2.9 Commentary Notes

It is in the commentary notes that editors usually find their voice. CNs give you the opportunity to highlight and explain issues in your play that you believe are important for the reader to be aware of; through your choices, you will be able to make a real difference to the reader's experience of the play. The series for which you are editing will have guidelines for the word count of CNs. Some series give scope for little more than glossarial-note-length comment; others may offer a larger total word count. Whatever word count you are granted, you will find that you are obliged to be more concise than you would prefer. We would encourage you to make a positive challenge out of the creation of CNs that provide the key information and interpretive possibilities within a minimal word count.

How you set about the process is up to you. Some editors (e.g., GM) prefer to build the commentary by sweeping through the entire text, taking one task at a time: to begin, for instance, with *OED* definitions, then to go through and gloss all classical references, and so on. Others (e.g., SG) prefer to work scene by scene, performing each of the necessary tasks in one go. Here are a few rules of thumb for writing CNs:

- Explain everything that needs explaining, whether or not previous editors have explained it, and especially if they haven't.
- Avoid extended paraphrasing wherever possible; if you do feel you need to paraphrase, then do so with a clear explanation of the source of difficulty.
- Keep the CN as brief as you can. You will probably have seen editions, especially of Shakespeare's plays, where a single page contains only one or two lines of the play, with the rest taken up with commentary notes and, below them, textual notes. A page of this kind may well explain

a crucial and knotty problem in the text and may demonstrate the editor's considerable erudition, but it can be a serious turn-off for the reader.
- Be careful in your own writing to avoid colloquial phrasing that some of your readers, especially if they live in another part of the world or belong to a different generation from you, may not readily understand.
- The relationship between CNs and the Introduction can be a challenge. Avoid repetition wherever possible. If something is extensively discussed in the Introduction, a CN may be brief and refer the reader to the pages in the Introduction where the issue is addressed. Readers, though, cannot be depended on to turn to the Introduction, so your note still must contain the minimum information to make sense of the lines and the action and to alert the reader to any issue at stake.

One important task of an editor creating CNs is to gloss difficult or unfamiliar words – typically providing concise definitions drawn from the *Oxford English Dictionary* – as well as words that have significantly altered their meaning over time. Remember that such words may not instantly appear 'hard' but may have meant something very different four hundred years ago from their meaning today. 'Mistress' and 'friend' are instances of words with connected meanings (each, depending on context, could mean the same as the modern word 'girlfriend') but with implications that have in effect reversed over time, the former in early modern writing not necessarily implying a sexual relationship, the latter in certain early modern contexts implying precisely that. Draw the reader's attention to the range of possible meanings of a word or phrase, as well as to syntactical nuances, to connotation, to wordplay. You may need at times to acquire knowledge of technical fields – from early modern fashion to theology, from foodstuffs to astronomy – that are not your normal territory. Much of the pleasure of editing stems from the frankly abstruse knowledge you accumulate in order to explain a given line for the reader. And do your best to avoid making 'common sense' or locally inflected assumptions about meanings rather than checking. Early modern references to birds and animals, for instance, can trip editors up. The word 'wagtail' may appear to mean 'a dog' (and has been glossed this way in editions) but is in fact the name for a common English bird; equally, the word 'buzzard' in an early modern English play refers to a hawk, not to the turkey vulture (which is not a European bird) to which the name was later given by British settlers in North America.

Gloss sexual and obscene words simply and directly.[45] Avoid coyness, but don't overdo the opposite: it is rarely necessary to gloss a word meaning vagina as 'cunt', as one edited volume did insistently some years ago, but do explain what is bawdy in 'bawdy talk'.[46] Don't treat every sexual innuendo (or what the *OED* calls 'coarse slang') as the primary meaning (e.g., 'prick' still means a dot, a puncture, to stab; the joke is usually that it *also* could mean penis). A wagtail remains a bird and only then 'a contemptuous term for a profligate or inconstant woman; hence, a prostitute, a courtesan' (*OED*). Editors also typically use CNs to gloss classical and Biblical references (normally for the latter citing from the Bishops' or Geneva Bibles that Shakespeare and his contemporaries had to hand and making use, e.g., of Shaheen 1999 and adjusting as necessary for plays outside the Shakespeare canon).[47] For proverbial language, see Dent 1981 or 1984 (unless Tilley 1951 offers a fuller account, as he sometimes does).[48] For explanation of issues relating to early modern English grammar as well as slang and non-English words and phrases, see Hope 2003 or Blake 2002.[49] Wiggins in association with Richardson 2012ff, updating Chambers, Bentley and others in respect of dating and other contextual issues, provides

---

[45] A helpful resource is Gordon Williams, *A Dictionary of Sexual Language and Imagery in Shakespeare and Stuart Literature* (Athlone Press, 1994).

[46] See Zachary Lesser 's chapter 'Country Matters' in *Hamlet after Q1: An Uncanny History of the Shakespearean Text* (University of Pennsylvania Press, 2015), pp. 72–114, for a model discussion.

[47] Naseeb Shaheen, *Biblical References in Shakespeare's Plays* (University of Delaware Press, 1999).

[48] R. W. Dent, *Shakespeare's Proverbial Language: An Index* (University of California Press, 1981); and *Proverbial Language in English Drama Exclusive of Shakespeare: An Index* (University of California Press, 1984). See also Morris Palmer Tilley, *A Dictionary of Proverbs in England in the Sixteenth and Seventeenth Centuries* (University of Michigan Press, 1951).

[49] Hope, *Shakespeare's Grammar*, and N. F. Blake, *A Grammar of Shakespeare's Language* (Red Globe Press, 2002).

mines of invaluable information.[50] Additionally, a CN is the place to expand on the contexts of key TNs, explaining substantive emendations to the base text, laying out the justification for the choices you have made as well as any cruxes that remain, and at times acknowledging the limitations of a given emendation. You may also explain the bibliographic problems that might have led to the need for emendation (difficulties of secretary hand, errors in casting off, the known preferences of a given compositor, etc.).

Otherwise, topics for CNs vary widely, based on the editor's interpretation and the subject matter and historical contexts of the play. While there is little value in unspecific descriptions of productions of your play, it is important to inform the reader about key moments in your play's afterlife on the stage (if it has one). Editors often describe how a particular moment was performed in a given production. We recommend, however, avoiding too many specifics about individual productions unless the interpretation in question becomes an unquestioned landmark in the play's performance history. In such cases, mentioning an actor or director by name becomes akin to naming the first editor to make a particular textual emendation. But beware the bias of the recent: remember that by the time the reader reads your edition, the current production you describe will already be firmly in the past. Nothing ages faster in an edition than its performance history, even if certain productions remain accessible by way, say, of streaming. This means that privileging a production you have recently seen and admired over landmark productions of a century earlier may not serve your reader unless one or the other participates in an argument or developing interpretation. The name of an actor who is a household name to you may mean nothing to your readers in ten years' time; equally, your favourite British or American actor may not be at all familiar to readers in another part of the world. Remember that your readers will have had very different experiences from you, not least of theatregoing, and the tendency for US- or UK-based editors to privilege

---

[50] Martin Wiggins, with Catherine Richardson, eds., *British Drama, 1533–1642: A Catalogue*, 9 vols to date (Oxford University Press, 2012-present). Older sources include E. K. Chambers, *The Elizabethan Stage*, 4 vols (Oxford University Press, 1923); and G. E. Bentley, *The Jacobean and Caroline Stage*, 7 vols (Clarendon Press, 1941–1956).

anglophone theatre history over global theatre *histories* serves to alienate and exclude readers beyond the anglophone sphere, not least in the Global South. Editors should aim to benefit from the considerable amount of scholarship produced over many decades on global productions of Shakespeare and other early modern playwrights. Remember too that, depending on your play and its relationship to a particular early modern company or playhouse, a discussion of the various roles that, say, Richard Burbage played for the King's Men or those of Nathan Field for the Children of the Queen's Revels may be valuable for discussion of your particular play.

Your own critical stance will encourage you to comment on issues that others might not note. Certainly, the historical moment in which you are working will mean that you may well write commentary notes on matters not only that previous editors have not noted but that you, too, had you been editing twenty years earlier, might not have thought to comment on. This is both why the work of Shakespeare and his contemporaries needs periodic re-editing as cultural and critical perspectives change and why editions do not last forever. (Realizing this is likely to make you kinder to your predecessors.) Terminology changes along with perspective. Certain terms traditionally used in discussion of *The Changeling*, for example, are simply no longer appropriate. The play's two narrative strands have long been known as the 'main plot' and the 'madhouse plot'; the *Oxford Middleton* did valuable service in re-naming these as the 'castle plot' and the 'hospital plot', thereby ensuring appropriate expression both for the play's dramatization of mental health and for the structural relationship between the two plots. Again, the castle plot pivots on a scene long referred to by critics and editors as the 'seduction scene'. The action in this scene is not a seduction; it is rape and should be so discussed. The editor has responsibilities in respect of such matters.

Discussion of prejudicial early modern representations of racial and cultural difference must be done both robustly and carefully – by no means a straightforward task, especially if you seek a diverse, global readership. The editor needs to be responsible, in other words, both to the play and to the edition's potential readers wherever they live and work or study. This can mean glossing words that earlier generations of editors have not glossed and doing so in the context of the current state of the critical field.

> Enter *Morochus* a tawnie Moore all in white, and three
> or foure followers accordingly, with *Portia*,
> *Nerriſſa*, and their traine.
> *Morocho.* Miſlike me not for my complexion,

Figure 22 William Shakespeare, Q *Merchant of Venice* B4ᵛ – STC 22296 copy 1, reproduced by kind permission of the Folger Shakespeare Library

Take the opening of *The Merchant of Venice* 2.1, for example. Figure 22 shows the beginning of the first of two brief scenes featuring the Prince of Morocco, the first of Portia's suitors that the audience encounters (quarto B4ᵛ). A glance at older editions will show that editors have typically chosen not to gloss '*Morochus*', 'tawnie', 'Moore', 'all in white', 'followers', 'traine' or 'complexion'. To a contemporary editor working in the context of premodern critical race studies, this is nigh on incomprehensible. The work of othering done by the play may operate for the most part in respect of Shylock, but the cultures of race and prejudice in the play's Belmont, by implication in the play's Venice, and at a further remove in Shakespeare's London are made very apparent as Morocco enters the scene. They are underlined by the reappearance of the word 'complexion' in the last line of his second and final scene, 2.7, in Portia's dismissive 'Let all of his complexion choose me so' (TLN 1053). The editor's responsibility in guiding the reader through this material encompasses the early modern past and the twenty-first-century present. Racism should be addressed as racism and should be situated in its early modern context – which will mean discussing the spelling of the name normally modernized to 'Morocco'; the racial, religious and geographical meanings of 'tawnie' and 'Moore'; the cultural implications of Shakespeare's choice to have Morocco, a Black man, enter 'all in white'; the implications of the choice of the word 'followers' for those accompanying Morocco and of 'traine' for those who accompany Portia; and the multiple meanings of 'complexion' (race, skin, physiology, the humours), as well as the four-syllable pronunciation ('com-plex-i-on') required by the metre and its possible implication that Morocco has a marked non-native-speaker accent. Given the nature of the play, it may well be that the editor will discuss the representation of Morocco in the Introduction, but it would seem essential to ensure that a reader who chooses not to read the Introduction is nonetheless provided with sufficient CNs to understand the range of meanings expressed in the stage direction and the scene's first line.

2.10 Critical/Textual Introduction

It is in the Introduction that you will offer your interpretation of the play most fully. If you have previously written a monograph or monographs, then the Introduction is likely to be where you, as a first-time editor, will feel most at home. At the same time, writing an Introduction to a critical edition is a very different game from writing a monograph because, unlike a monograph with a specific focus, an Introduction needs to cover *all* the necessary bases. As with the CNs, the Introduction is not simply a locus for your discussion of issues in which you have a particular critical interest; rather, you are aiming to offer the reader a genuine overview of the main issues raised by the play, and you have a limited word count in which to do so. Depending on the series for which you are editing, you may have as many as 25,000 words to work with – not much less than the length of this *Element* – but because of the sheer range of topics you will need to address, and because if you are to engage and inform your readers you will need to write elegantly, without cramming overmuch information into compressed sentences, you will rapidly realize how tight this figure is. Just like an efficient TN or CN, a good Introduction to a critical edition is a model of conciseness.

If you take a look at editions of early modern plays from the mid twentieth century, you will see that their Introductions followed a near-universal pattern, one normally organized by these headings: Date, Author(s), First Performance, Sources, The Play (subdivided into sections such as Form, Style, Characters, Dramatic Vision, Criticism, Achievement), Theatre Productions, The Text. The sections on 'The Play' are usually the most visibly dated. If you then turn to editions from the last twenty or thirty years, you will see not only that editors have typically written with a critical currency that supersedes Author-centred concepts such as 'Dramatic Vision' and 'Achievement' but have also felt able to vary the standard organizational pattern, still addressing each of the key topics but arranging them in a way that best suits their play. This might, for instance, mean beginning with the performance history, if the play in question has had particular prominence on the stage or if, say, it was a major play on the nineteenth-century stage but is now rarely performed, such as *Henry VIII*. Or it might mean, if the play has a particularly provocative textual history – *Hamlet*, most obviously – beginning not, as you might expect, with the play's critical and performance history but with a question of the text. Varying the traditional order of the introduction may also have the considerable value of enabling an editor right from the outset to differentiate her work from that of her predecessors and to make clear how her particular perspective is going to provide new insight into a well-known play.

Take a look, for instance, at three exemplary critical editions from the 2000s: Martin Butler's New Cambridge Shakespeare edition of *Cymbeline*, John Jowett's Oxford Shakespeare edition of *Richard III*, and Clare McManus's edition of John Fletcher's *The Island Princess* for Arden Early Modern Drama.[51] Butler begins with a paragraph that confronts head on certain persistently negative critical attitudes towards *Cymbeline* – that it is too long and cumbersome; that its characterization is stilted; that it is dramaturgically clunky, especially in its final scene; that it was written by a supposedly ageing Shakespeare losing his creative focus – attitudes that had dogged the play for decades by the time Butler edited it. He rejects these attitudes immediately. The play's 'capaciousness is its great virtue', he insists, robustly describing Posthumus as an 'innocent prude', Cloten as a 'refined brute' and Iachimo's behaviour as 'corrosive cynicism', and directly asserting that the play 'was produced by a dramatist working at the height of his powers'.[52] He then organizes the rest of his Introduction broadly within the standard frame, but bringing genre, influence, historical context, the way the play dramatizes women's experience, and its

---

[51] *Cymbeline*, ed. Martin Butler, 'New Cambridge Shakespeare' (Cambridge University Press, 2005); *Richard III*, ed. John Jowett (Oxford University Press, 2003); John Fletcher, *The Island Princess*, ed. Clare McManus (Bloomsbury Arden Shakespeare, 2012).

[52] *Cymbeline*, ed. Butler, p. 1.

performance history to the fore prior to offering his overall interpretation – a traditional approach, in a way, and certainly one that covers the ground, but also marking both his own critical currency and his resolute determination to prove the play's detractors wrong.

Jowett, editing a canonical play in less need of reparative critical defence, begins boldly by twinning performance and metadrama: '*Richard III* is conspicuously a performance piece', he announces, 'and in many ways it is about performance'.[53] He then arranges his Introduction in four sections that do not look at all like the traditional structure, though they do in fact cover traditional ground: 'Taking Shape' (encompassing date, company, genre, sources and historical context), 'Episodes on the Edge of History' (broadly speaking covering what might once have been in the section called 'The Play'), 'On Stage' (performance history) and 'In Print' (textual introduction). Jowett's Introduction, in other words, refreshes the reader's engagement with *Richard III* and celebrates the play even as it addresses all the necessary elements and offers a genuinely new set of perspectives.

McManus's edition and her introduction do very different work from those of Butler and Jowett because, rather than re-presenting a canonical text that has been the subject of multiple critical editions, she is seeking to insert a new play, one that will in all probability be wholly new to the reader, into the teaching canon of early modern drama. Her task, then, is to make a case for an unknown text and its relevance for twenty-first-century readers while at the same time covering the critical ground essential for any serious critical edition. She begins by situating the play in respect of two much better-known plays, *The Tempest* and *Othello*, to give the reader familiar comparison points, and she makes it clear that she will engage with key cultural and historical issues: the global, gender, race, empire and religion. She notes both the play's sustained popularity on the stage until the mid-eighteenth-century and the 'striking topicality' of its politics – its representation of what she calls 'the imperial encounter of Muslim and Christian' – for 'the post-9/11 moment'.[54] The organization of her Introduction – the play, sources, genre, historical contexts, performance history, text – follows the traditional path, but the foci

[53] Jowett, ed., *Richard III*, 1. [54] McManus, ed., *The Island Princess*, 5.

of her 'play' section ('eros and faith', 'the geography of romance', 'theatrical women and the staging of desire'), of her 'sources' section ('theatre across borders'), of her 'performance' section ('staging the east') and of her 'text' section ('the gender of editing') together make clear her critical perspective on the play and its challenges.

As these examples suggest, a well-written Introduction will be vibrant, imaginative, alive to the critical moment and appropriate to the play's place in cultural, critical, performance and textual history. At the same time, an Introduction, by definition, needs to include certain topics, which are usually these:

- A best guess for the date of composition, including any date-delimiting allusions in the text. If this involves a complex argument, it is probably better to publish it elsewhere or in a Longer Note. It is now standard to cite the dating proposed in Wiggins and Richardson's compendious *Catalogue*.[55]
- The date of the first performance (if known), along with records of early performances (if any), information about the acting company and about the theatre(s) in which the play was performed.
- Any available information about the original cast and about possible doubling of roles so as to give your reader a sense of the minimum number of actors required to perform the play as printed. You may wish to include a doubling chart as an appendix.
- Discussion of the other plays by your playwright(s), of other relevant plays performed by the same company, and of the influence of your play on later plays.
- As comprehensive a list of sources as you can provide, along with an analysis of the way they have been deployed and adapted for the play. Depending on their availability elsewhere, you may wish to reproduce key passages in an appendix.
- Evidence of authorship or of collaboration if your play is multiply authored, to include data from attributional analysis as available.

---

[55] Martin Wiggins, in association with Catherine Richardson, *British Drama 1533–1642: A Catalogue*, 9 vols to date (Oxford University Press, 2011).

Editing an Early Modern Play 71

- Historical contexts, both of the moments in which your play was written and first performed and of relevant subsequent moments in its afterlife. Remember: many of your readers may well be a lot hazier than you about Elizabethan and Jacobean history, never mind about the Georgian, Victorian or Edwardian periods, and you need to help them, quietly and minimally, to get a toehold.
- Performance history, to include discussion of particulars of the earliest productions, use of music, say, or props or parts of the stage such as the balcony or 'trap', and a survey of relevant productions from the play's first appearance to current stage or screen versions (if any). Include only those productions that you believe are landmarks in the play's stage history or that foreground aspects of the play that might otherwise have remained hidden. This may well require you to develop a sense of the key developments in theatre history over a period of centuries. If the play you are editing, like many by playwrights other than Shakespeare, has little modern production history, you may nevertheless want to discuss any staging problems the play presents: for example, how was the workshop of *Shoemaker's Holiday* or of *Eastward Ho!* presented on the early modern stage? Was a bed 'thrust out' in *Sophonisba* and in *Othello*? How did Juno 'descend' in *The Tempest*? What does the single-word SD 'Diana' mean in *Pericles*?
- Critical history, to include issues from race to gender, genre to politics, disability to the supernatural – wherever your play and your own critical perspective takes you. This is the section of your Introduction in which you can most readily stamp your identity on the edition. But remember two things: your word count is severely limited, and you are writing not for yourself or for three or four academics whose work you admire but for your potential readers in all their range and diversity.
- Either as part of the Introduction or in an appendix (our preference, though, is *not* to relegate the textual introduction to the status of an appendix), you will discuss the text, describing the significant characteristics of your base text, explaining what seems to you or other textual critics to be the nature of the manuscript behind it, the stages of its production, and the choices you have made in creating your edition.

This is by no means a comprehensive list of everything that the Introduction to a critical edition may include. But it does give you a framework with which to think about the kinds of information and interpretation your reader will benefit from as they encounter the play for the first time. The joy of twenty-first-century editing is that editors now have a great deal of creative and critical freedom in the writing of Introductions. But your Introduction will not be complete if you do not cover the necessary topics. Readers will turn to your edition for an informed opinion on issues such as authorship, sources and the date of first performance: certainly you cannot omit these things, nor should you make them difficult to find. In other words, avoid so idiosyncratic a structure for your Introduction that the basic information for which readers typically turn to an edition's Introduction is effectively hidden from them.

Finally, many series suggest that you become an advocate for your play – as Butler does overtly in the first paragraph of his Introduction. This role has particular value when you are editing a play by Shakespeare that has been downplayed in critical history or, still more so, one by a dramatist other than Shakespeare, not least because your readers are far less likely to have seen performances of, say, *The Shoemaker's Holiday*, *Philaster* or *The Malcontent* than they are of the major Shakespeare plays, and they need to be shown why these plays are important both in themselves and in dramatic and critical history. It is not absolutely always the case, though, that editors insist on singing the praises of their play, and there may be value at times in making it apparent that you retain a certain critical distance from the object of your edition. Sometimes you edit a play because you think it important that a critical edition, or even just an edition, exist.[56] Usually, though, you take on a play because you think the world of it, or you take it on because you have been asked to do so and the more you immerse yourself in it, the more you find you love it – or, if you don't, then the more intrigued you become about why, for instance, it appears to have been a highly popular play in its day. Asking such questions will be immensely instructive both for you and for your readers.

---

[56] As was the case with the plays SG found in the English College, Rome.

2.11 Concluding Advice

It is only over when it is over. When you send everything to your general editor (assuming you have one), brace yourself. Your work is not finished at this point, not by a long chalk. Nobody – not the most experienced editor – gets everything right in the first draft, and if you are editing for the first time, then you will inevitably have made a certain number of errors and omissions. If you are editing for a series such as Arden or Cambridge, you will already have created a sample scene or act so that your general editor could catch potential problems at an early stage. But every edition includes errors, and we urge you to be grateful to, not annoyed with, your general editor, when she offers constructive feedback. If you are editing for print publication, remember that your text is very unlikely to be copyedited to the degree that was once the norm, and that your general editor's reading will probably be the most careful your typescript will receive. We cannot resist quoting Clifford Leech at this point:

> In all probability, your general editor is underpaid and tired; he believes in his job and expects you to believe in yours; there is no point in losing your temper with him (every editor may feel so inclined on occasion): he may well have restrained himself rather hard before deciding that he must not lose his temper with you. The remarkable thing is that, in the end, friendship between editor and general editor tends to grow through the joint task; in few instances is there an ultimate falling-out. But patience on both sides will at times be needed.[57]

The pronouns may have changed since 1970, but the tensions – and the friendships that can result from shared endeavour – have not.

When the proofs are scheduled, make sure you create ample time – by which we mean several days – to check them. They cannot be rushed. Try to find a way to read the proofs that will not lead you back into the materials as you know them – thus, instead of reading a scene at a time, read a page.

---

[57] Leech, '*On Editing*', p. 62.

Try reading difficult passages backwards. Read everything over and over, especially parts of the volume that you or someone in the publishing house added late in the game – the table of contents, the acknowledgements, the running heads that appear at the top of each page, even advertising copy. Many errors occur in paratext inserted late and not read and sometimes not even seen by the editor. Check the scene and line numbers that appear, typically, as identifiers at the top of a page. Be sure you know whether your guidelines direct you to put the number of a split line with the second or the first section and go through and recheck each one. If your play is in a series, keep not only the guidelines but an earlier volume close by and constantly available so that you can check the formatting. Remember – and you may not have seen this coming – that in the change from your submitted document to typesetting, the line numbers of prose will change, and all references to those lines will need to change too (unless you are lucky enough to be editing a digital edition with a platform that ensures that line numbers don't change in prose passages). This means you must re-count the lines in *every* scene, probably more than once, and then you must correct *all* references in your text, TNs, CNs and Introduction to the new numbers – which is, frankly, a significantly tedious and time-consuming process. But be completely unyielding about these things. You do not want a picky reviewer of your edition (and they exist, believe us) providing a lengthy list of errata. Aim to give that reviewer little or nothing to work with. Once again, we urge you to do what used to be the work of copy editors. Are your brief one-or-two-word glosses supposed to end with a full stop? How many spaces form an indent? Are split lines properly staircased? Even the most careful of editors may forget whether the second half of a line of verse accompanies its speech prefix or belongs below it.

The result of all this work will be a critical edition of which you can be proud, knowing the care and belief you have put into it.

This, then, is (a very brief account of) the practice of editing an early modern play – or at least it is our shared take on that practice. It will no doubt be clear by now that editing is a time-consuming and intellectually demanding task but also, assuming you are intellectually curious and keen to acquire a new scholarly skillset, a profoundly exciting one to have ahead of you. If you now go on to edit a critical edition of an early modern play, you will, we guarantee, develop, expand and improve your critical capacity beyond measure.

There is, though, as we have repeatedly said, no practice without theory, and so now we will turn, if necessarily briefly, to the latter.

3 Theory

There is no practice without theory. Editing practice is no different. We chose to organize this Element in what might seem the wrong order, beginning (and continuing for the bulk of the book) with practice and ending with theory, but we did so deliberately. This Element is first and foremost a brief practical guide designed to introduce the first-time editor, and anyone curious about the business of editing, to the essentials of the task. But an introduction of this kind cannot be only practical; it must also engage with the textual theories that underpin the practice, theories that are both fascinating and, we believe, fundamental to a scholarly understanding of early modern play texts. We conclude this Element, then, by briefly addressing some basic tenets of textual theory while also making it clear that textual theory is, above all, a *theory of practice* and is thus not precisely the same as – although it overlaps with and is substantially indebted to – other forms of literary theory.

As we noted in the previous section, the challenge that faces all editors of early modern plays is the fragmentary nature of what has come down to us in physical form from four hundred years ago. Editors must infer the nature of the absent manuscript from the printed page. The question is what you then do with the inferences you have made, what kind of edition you choose to create, what moment in the history of the text you seek to instantiate in your edition, and, at a fundamental level, what your understanding is of the way creative texts come into being. It is these questions that textual theory addresses. We cannot here offer a thoroughgoing history of textual theory. If you wish to pursue these issues further, we recommend that you take a look at the following recent volumes (for details, see the 'Further Reading' list, where we provide references both to work we cite and to a range of further useful materials): John Jowett, *Shakespeare and Text*; Gabriel Egan, *The Struggle for Shakespeare's Text*; Margaret Jane Kidnie and Sonia Massai (eds.), *Shakespeare and Textual Studies*; Claire M. L. Bourne (ed.), *Shakespeare/Text: Contemporary Readings in Textual Studies, Editing and Performance*; Lukas Erne (ed.), *The Arden Research Handbook of Shakespeare and Textual Studies*; and Suzanne Gossett, *Shakespeare and Textual Theory*. These are only a handful of the many excellent monographs, handbooks and edited collections on the subject of editorial theory and practice that address, eloquently and in depth, the issues we touch on. There is also a great deal of foundational work by scholars named repeatedly in these recent accounts – revered names such as W. W. Greg, Alfred Hart, Charlton Hinman, E. A. J. Honigmann, R. B. McKerrow, Alfred W. Pollard, Fredson Bowers and others – all of whose work will be of immense value to anyone thinking about editing an early modern play. The word count for an Element means we have omitted mention of many books and essays we would have wished to cite. But to those we have mentioned, we would add one more recent volume: Clare Loffman and Harriet Phillips's *Handbook of Editing Early Modern Texts*.[58] We do so because so much of the work we have cited addresses Shakespeare and all of it addresses drama, whereas Loffman and Phillips include drama among a wide range of kinds of early modern text from manuscript to print, from poetry to prose. The usual divisions – both between Shakespeare and everyone else and between printed drama and other genres – are unfortunately symptomatic of a fragmented field, one distorted by the cultural hegemony of the figure of Shakespeare, and by a regrettable absence of dialogue between Shakespeareans and editors of other kinds of early modern text apart from those of other dramatists. We realize that, in focusing for this Element on the editing of early modern drama, we are sustaining aspects of this division, and we will not defend this other than to say that we have written about what we know best and that, in a certain way, the practical aim of our book is most closely matched to that of Loffman and Phillips.

We will now turn to certain key aspects of textual theory as they emerge from the practice we have described. Please bear in mind that the upcoming account expresses our own perspective on these matters and that others may

---

[58] *A Handbook of Editing Early Modern Texts: Material Readings in Early Modern Culture*, eds. Clare Loffman and Harriet Phillips (Routledge, 2020).

well differ from us, perhaps vehemently, on fundamental issues. We urge you to read widely in establishing your own position.

3.1 Textual Theory

What *is* **textual theory?** The term (along with 'textual criticism') is often used loosely and vaguely to mean a conjunction of some kind between literary theory and textual analysis. This is not helpful. Textual theory, as we describe it, is unconnected to textual analysis in the sense of close reading, practical criticism or other formalistic interpretive practices. Rather, textual theory provides the theoretical framework for thinking about the material text: it is the set of abstract principles structuring the conjectures scholars make as they try to understand the implications of print or manuscript materials and negotiate certain challenges those materials present, a set of principles aimed at informing and establishing practice. Traditionally, for Shakespeare and early modern theatre studies, textual theory has meant a methodology, one constructed with an approximation to scientific rigour, for inferring the nature of an absent manuscript from a text printed from that manuscript, an inference that is understood as the key determining factor in the choices made by an editor preparing the text. Exponents of this version of textual theory – notably those belonging to the key twentieth-century school known as the **New Bibliography** – sought first and foremost to exclude anything they viewed as extrinsic to the original creator's (or creators') work. What mattered was to find rigorous ways to peel back the layers of material history (to 'lift the veil', to cite a still more problematic metaphor of depth and discovery) between Shakespeare's moment and the present day, to uncover by inference the text as it was when the author completed it, and (in the purest form of New Bibliography) to treat all other interventions, all other agencies, as phenomena to be identified precisely so that they could be sidelined. Textual theory in this sense emerged as a theory of textual **intention**, one designed to inform the practice of the editor through a practical process that rigorously privileges the **Author.**

As G. Thomas Tanselle phrased it in a set of lectures published in 1989, '[e]very verbal text, whether spoken or written down, is an attempt to convey a work'.[59] By 'work' he means something that exists in the author's imagination prior to and **extrinsic** to any material manifestation of that work. A work, he argues, 'is an ineluctable entity', whereas 'a reproduction' (all material texts are, for Tanselle, reproductions of a work) 'is an approximation, forever open to question and always tempting one to remedial action'.[60] Yet a 'text', it seems, can also be intangible; it too can exist in the mind of the author. 'We need to distinguish in some way between the texts of a work as they existed in the mind where it originated and the texts of that work that contain contributions by others', he proposes, adding that 'one shorthand way of referring to this distinction is to say that the former are the texts the author intended and that the latter may in some ways conform to what the author expected'. This leads Tanselle into a complex place in respect of intentions: 'Like other people', he notes,

> authors can be expected to change their minds; and whether they write out whole texts when they make revisions or enter the revisions on pre-existing documents or hold them in their minds, the intention underlying the altered phrases is of the same order as that underlying the previous version of them. [61]

The particular challenge Tanselle addresses here – the existence of multiple authorial versions of a poem or novel by a given writer – is one that is somewhat oblique to the challenges faced by the editor of an early modern play, given the absence of dramatic manuscripts and the paucity of plays for which there is more than one early text. Yet the overall point he makes – that the editor's concern is to produce a text that conforms to the author's intentions – was the basic premise of New Bibliography, and it was tested out in the first instance on early modern play texts.

Theories of the text (note the plural) are, however, far more all-encompassing than this brief sketch of New Bibliography suggests. They

---

[59] G. Thomas Tanselle, *A Rationale of Textual Criticism* (University of Pennsylvania Press, 2009), p. 68.
[60] Tanselle, *Rationale*, p. 14. [61] Tanselle, *Rationale*, pp. 78–79.

are, in David Greetham's words, 'theories of writing and of reading, theories of intention and of reception, theories of transmission and of corruption, and theories of originary conception and of social consumption and variation'.[62] By the time Tanselle outlined at the end of the 1980s his own distillation of work begun by scholars across the twentieth century – above all, W. W. Greg, the key figure in early New Bibliography – critical attitudes beyond his particular bibliographical sphere had already changed substantially and had begun significantly to affect the business of editing, in effect undoing the decoupling of scholarship (understood as the field encompassed by bibliography, history of the book and editing) from criticism that had been effected early in the century. Not only, it was now argued, can '[n]o single version of a literary work, whether Renaissance or modern, ... offer us the fond dream of unmediated access to an author', but our attention should be directed at least as much to the mediation as to the role of the author.[63] The most influential rethinking of editorial theory emerged as the sociology of the text, a school of thought that rejected the key binary articulated by Tanselle – 'the texts of a work as they existed in the mind where it originated' and 'the texts of that work that contain contributions by others'[64] – and argued that excluding the latter in favour of the (imaginary) former is to misunderstand the multiple *social* agencies that combine to create a text.

The central impetus for the sociology of the text was the questioning of the long-standing hegemony within textual studies of a Romantic conception of authorship, a process initiated in the late 1960s by prominent poststructuralists, above all Roland Barthes ('The Death of the Author') and Michel Foucault ('What is an Author?'). The latter argued that the author should be understood not as a named individual whose single imagination generates, and controls the meaning of, the text but instead as a 'principle of thrift in the proliferation of meaning', that is, as a concept

---

[62] D. C. Greetham, *Textual Scholarship: An Introduction* (Clarendon Press, 1999), p. 1.

[63] Leah S. Marcus, *Unediting the Renaissance: Shakespeare, Marlowe, Milton* (Routledge, 1996), p. 3.

[64] Tanselle, *Rationale*, p. 78.

created to impose a particular set of boundaries (the writer's life span, say) within which the text, otherwise unbounded in its significations, might be comprehended.[65] Once the figure of the author is reimagined in this way, the concept of the 'work' – understood as the unsullied precursor of the text as it existed at a certain moment in the mind of the author – comes under extreme pressure. For one key exponent of the sociology of the text, D. F. McKenzie, the history of the book – analysing, for example, the role of publishers in creating meaning across publication contexts and markets and in conjunction with designers, printers and readers – makes the idea of the single authoritative edition untenable.[66] For another, Jerome McGann (whose arguments, he insists, derive from book history, not poststructuralism), the focus of critical attention becomes not 'the author' but 'that complex network of people, materials, and events which have produced and which continue to reproduce the literary works which history delivers into our hands'[67] – a statement that firmly redefines the 'work' as collaborative in the broadest sense.

It was Stephen Orgel, in a brief essay called 'What is a Text?', who had first set out – eight years before Tanselle's lectures were published – the implications of the rejection of the author as the sole arbiter of meaning for the study of Shakespeare and early modern drama. In doing so, he made it apparent that certain key issues that consistently frustrated the New Bibliographers – above all, the instability of the early modern dramatic text and the multiple agencies engaged in the various collaborative processes that led to that text – might be viewed not as regrettable but, on the contrary, as phenomena to celebrate. 'We assume', he notes, 'that the

---

[65] Michel Foucault, 'What is an Author', in *The Book History Reader*, eds. David Finkelstein and Alistair McCleery, 2nd ed. (Routledge, 2006), pp. 281–291 (290).

[66] D. F. McKenzie, *Bibliography and the Sociology of Texts* (Cambridge University Press, 2004; first published by the British Library, 1985); and 'History of the Book', in *The Book Encompassed*, ed. Peter Davison (Cambridge University Press, 1992), pp. 290–301.

[67] Jerome McGann, *The Beauty of Inflections: Literary Investigations in Historical Method and Theory* (Oxford University Press, 1988), p. 80.

authority of a text derives from the author', and he then proceeds: 'Self-evident as it may appear, I suggest that this proposition is not true: in the case of Renaissance dramatic texts it is almost never true'.[68] He cites the textual scholar E. A. J. Honigmann, who 'shows quite persuasively that the notion of final or complete versions assumed by virtually all modern editors of Shakespeare is inconsistent with everything we know not only about Renaissance theatrical practice, but about the way writers in fact work', and he adds that 'virtually all theatrical literature must be seen as basically collaborative in nature'.[69] Thus he suggests that if Shakespeare is to be distinguished from other playwrights, it is 'only because he was in on more parts of the collaboration' by virtue of his unique role with the King's Men.[70]

What does all of this mean for the editor?

One major impact the sociology of the text has had on editing practice is in the understanding of the base text. How do you infer the manuscript copy on which it was based? Which moment in the history of the text are you reproducing? The New Bibliographers had a well-documented tendency to think in binaries, and a key binary in their conceptualizing of the underlying copy of a given printed text was either 'foul papers', defined as an authorial rough draft that could be expected to contain errors, loosenesses, cancellations and so on, or 'fair copy', understood as the author's (or a scribe's) neatly written-out version adequately conforming to an author's 'final intentions'. But this binary is simply not sufficient to describe the variable transmission processes that seem to have taken place among playwright, acting company and printer. Thus, instead of one simple sequence – a playwright writes a script and hands it to an acting company – there could be other interventions between the writer and the surviving texts, some that almost reverse this order. For example, based on characteristic

---

[68] Stephen Orgel, 'What Is a Text?', in *Research Opportunities in Renaissance Drama* 24 (1981), pp. 3–6 (3); reprinted in Orgel, *The Authentic Shakespeare, and Other Problems of the Early Modern Stage* (Routledge, 2002), pp. 20–25.

[69] Orgel, 'What Is a Text?', p. 6, citing E. A. J. Honigmann, *The Stability of Shakespeare's Text* (Arnold, 1965).

[70] Orgel, 'What Is a Text?', p. 6.

errors, it has been argued that some dramatic texts may have been taken down in shorthand during performance, as was often the case with sermons in the period, and then expanded for publication. In this case, the history of the surviving text, rather than being the playwright's manuscript followed by printed text, might be manuscript, spoken text, new manuscript and only then print, providing a range of opportunities for error. Furthermore, the company was obliged to give a fair copy to the Master of the Revels for his approval. Since that copy, when returned, would have his licence on it, the company would be loath to part with it, making it unlikely that this copy was given to the printer. Hence a further copy would be needed – but would it be identical with the copy that had been approved, and perhaps annotated, by the Master? Some surviving texts occasionally contain the names of actors rather than characters, which may mean either that the playwright was, pre-performance, envisioning one of his peers in a given role while he was writing that role – collaborating, in a certain sense, with that actor – or, on the contrary, that the manuscript on which the printed text is based had been annotated by the bookkeeper in the wake of performance. At almost any point in the progress from writer to printed text there may have been revisions, whether authorial or theatrical. We know far less than we would like to about the textual ecosystems of the early modern stage and about how publishers acquired the copy for the play texts they published. But where this was the cause of immense frustration for a textual scholar intent on 'lifting the veil' to determine an author's final intentions, for someone working in the wake of the changes of perception effected by the conjunction of textual theory with poststructuralism it can instead be something to be appreciated and explored.

The sociology of the text demonstrates that textual theory intersects with other forms of theoretical inquiry, not least with theories of exclusion of various kinds. An editor seeks to make the text *accessible* by way of her edition, but to whose work is she providing access? And to whose work might she be unintentionally denying access? The history of the book makes it clear that books police their readers. All editions do so in effect by the decisions they make about what to explain and what to assume is apparent, about what to include and what to exclude. The canon of a given playwright is one of the most obvious contexts for inclusion and exclusion.

Editing an Early Modern Play 83

Attribution scholarship has in recent decades expanded the Shakespeare canon, taking in entire plays such as *Edward III* and finding collaborators in plays from *Macbeth* to *All's Well That Ends Well*, and editions have followed suit, making it very clear that the plays in the Shakespeare canon embody the work of more than one writer.[71] In foregrounding shared agency in the creation of the printed object, the sociology of the text bridged the gap – which by this time had become substantial – between the practice of editing and that of critical theory in the various forms in which it had emerged by the 1980s and 1990s.

In other words, the phenomena that New Bibliographers set aside so as to focus on the author and his work – phenomena such as the activities of collaborating writers, of actors, of scribes, of the theatre company, of compositors, of publishers, of adapters and so on – became objects of critical engagement. This turn to multiple agency challenged the singular focus of the New Bibliographers on the Author, but it also had the effect of privileging their unquestioned achievements in understanding the material processes that together produce the text, along with those of bibliography in general, which in McKenzie's words is

> the only discipline which has consistently studied the composition, formal design and transmission of texts by writers, printers, and publishers; their distribution through different communities by wholesalers, retailers, and teachers; their collection and classification by librarians; their meaning for, and ... their creative regeneration by, readers.[72]

Thus an editor in the wake of the sociology of the text may not agree with certain *premises* of the work performed by the New

---

[71] The theatrical world's continued insistence on the number 'thirty-seven' for the plays of Shakespeare – even as certain Shakespeare-centred theatres perform plays that fall outside the normal count, such as *The Two Noble Kinsmen* – suggests that scholarly work on authorial attribution has yet to have much of an impact on the cultural edifice known as 'Shakespeare'.

[72] McKenzie, *Bibliography*, p. 12.

Bibliographers – particularly the wholesale privileging of the author over other agents in the transmission of a text – but she will profoundly appreciate the work itself, since it so rigorously delineates the roles played by those non-authorial agents. There never was, in truth, a clear caesura between the era of the New Bibliography and that following the emergence of the sociology of the text.[73] The tensions between scholars primarily focused on the author and those fascinated by multiple agency continue to make themselves felt in debates today, not least in authorial attribution studies. Why do we aim to differentiate between collaborators, and on what basis do we do so? Must individual scenes in a play always be assumed to be the work of one or the other collaborator? Might playwrights not have worked together on a given scene? And, if so, what does this mean for the techniques of authorial attribution, which bring to bear a positivism that arguably runs counter to the philosophical tendencies of most literary critics? The insertion of the term 'co-author' into debates about attribution (as opposed to terms that avoid the loaded word 'author' – 'collaborator', say, or the early modern term 'coadjutor') suggests a backlash.

The moment of the sociology of the text was, and remains, one of tension between defenders of the New Bibliography and the French-theory-inspired scholars who assaulted some of the most cherished intellectual premises of their immediate predecessors. But it was at the same time a moment at which key bridges were formed between editors and critics, facilitating a recognition by each of the value to be found in each other's respective knowledge sets. For all the ways in which certain principles of the New Bibliography have, over decades now, been subject to critique, it would be absurd to deny that editors continue to depend in fundamental ways on the work of the New Bibliographers as they assess how, say, their base text was printed. No matter how much an editor may disagree with the stance of the Virginia School on the subject of authorial intentionality, she may have reason to be very grateful indeed for the work of members of that

---

[73] For discussion, see Gabriel Egan, *The Struggle for Shakespeare's Text: Twentieth-Century Editorial Theory and Practice* (Cambridge University Press, 2010), pp. 129–166.

school – that of Charlton Hinman, say, on print shop processes. (It was Hinman who painstakingly demonstrated that no two copies of the Shakespeare First Folio are identical.[74]) Many achievements, if not all of the working premises, of the New Bibliography remain, and all editors are indebted to them.

3.2 Intersections

In the preface, we listed several areas of intellectual engagement in which an editor will need to become knowledgeable. These included not only bibliographical methodologies for establishing a reliable text but also critical approaches that are most appropriate for situating the play for your readers. It is the responsibility of a twenty-first-century editor to produce a twenty-first-century edition, which means learning from, and bringing into your practice, aspects of, for example, feminism, critical race studies, queer theory, performance theory, disability studies, emotion studies and so on, as the play and your own critical orientation seem to you to suggest. It is important too to realize that a particular critical perspective can intersect with the theory and practice of editing in ways that can be hugely productive – as the intersection of poststructuralism and textual criticism in the 1980s and 1990s turned out to be.

We will briefly describe three examples of such intersections. One is an instance of an intersection between textual studies and feminist criticism; another between textual studies and queer theory; and the third between textual studies and premodern critical race studies. Each demonstrates the value both textual and critical that can emerge from the work that is done in convergence.

In 1978, a scholar called Jeanne Addison Roberts undertook a little textual sleuthing so as to intervene in a long-standing debate about a crux in *The Tempest*. In the course of the masque scene, 4.1, Ferdinand, enchanted by the visions Prospero has conjured up, exclaims: 'Let me liue here euer, / So rare a wondred Father and a wise / Makes this place Paradise' (TLN 1785–7) (see Figure 23). Editors had long felt that Ferdinand, in making

---

[74] Charlton Hinman, *The Printing and Proof-Reading of the First Folio of Shakespeare* (Oxford University Press, 1963).

> *Fer.* Let me liue here euer,
> So rare a wondred Father, and a wife
> Makes this place Paradife.

Figure 23 William Shakespeare, F *Tempest* TLN 1785-7 – RBD EL SH15M 1623, reproduced by kind permission of the Free Library of Philadelphia, Rare Book Department

such a fuss about his soon-to-be father-in-law, is being a little graceless in respect of his fiancée. Nicolas Rowe in 1709 chose to emend 'wise' to 'wife' on two grounds: one, his sense of social propriety; two, his hypothesis that the Folio compositor had misread an 'f' as a long 's', an easy error to make. (Neither 'wise' nor 'wife' creates an ideal rhyme with 'paradise'.) Most subsequent editors reverted to 'wise' on the grounds that the Folio printed an 's', not an 'f', noting that the reading 'wise' did not obviously require emendation. Roberts, however, working in the heyday of feminist scholarship, re-examined multiple copies of the Folio in the Folger Shakespeare Library and believed she found two (numbers 6 and 73) in which the letter appeared to be not a long 's' but an 'f' and then two more in which it appeared that the crossbar of the 'f' was in the process of breaking off.[75] As a result, some editors, returning to Rowe's choice, began to emend 'wise' to 'wife', and Miranda's inclusion in Ferdinand's vision of the perfect life seemed confirmed. The debate, however, did not stop there. Counterarguments have subsequently been made, from the claim that the 'crossbar' Roberts found is not in fact part of the type but something extraneous that was soon brushed away by the printing process or was merely minor ink blotting (Blayney) to an objection that reading 'wife' for 'wise' creates 'a profoundly different passage ... on ideological grounds' (Loughnane).[76] As the latter suggests, grounds for refuting textual claims do not, and cannot, always remain purely

---

[75] Jeanne Addison Roberts, '"Wife" or "wise" – *The Tempest*, l. 1786', *Studies in Bibliography* 31 (1978): 203–208 (206–207).

[76] Peter W. M. Blayney, 'Introduction to the Second Edition', in *The Norton Facsimile: The First Folio of Shakespeare*, ed. Charlton Hinman (W. W. Norton, 1996), pp. xxvii–xxxvii; Rory Loughnane, ed., *The Tempest*, in *The New Oxford*

textual; bibliography and critical interpretation inevitably overlap. In this instance, even if bibliographical evidence does not ultimately support Roberts's claim, the feminist impetus that sent her to the Folger nonetheless reawakened interest in this long-standing crux. A similar impetus helped SG resolve a crux in *Pericles*. The quarto has Dionyza say she will tell Pericles, when he asks for his child, 'that shee is dead. Nurses are not the fates to foster it, not euer to preserve', garbled phrasing that had puzzled editors for centuries. Here, a combination of feminism and textual scholarship – the acquisition of knowledge of Jacobean childrearing and nursing practices together with bibliographical awareness that type could move during printing – led to a simple textual adjustment: 'Nurses are not the fates. To foster is not ever to preserve'.

Our second example lies at the intersection between textual scholarship and queer theory. In the previous section, we commented on 'mistress' and 'friend' as instances of connected words with implications that have in effect reversed over time, 'mistress' in an early modern context not necessarily implying a sexual relationship, 'friend' implying precisely that. It is to the word 'friend' that Jeffrey Masten turns in outlining the implication of what he calls 'queer philology' for the practice of editing and in particular for the challenges presented by the gloss or commentary note. The instance he takes is a gloss in *The Norton Shakespeare*, *Third Edition* of a word in *The Merchant of Venice*. Lorenzo, praising Portia for her forbearance in coping with Bassanio's absence while he has gone to help Antonio, says this:

> But if you knew to whom you show this honour,
> How true a gentleman you send relief,
> How dear a lover of my lord your husband,
> I know you would be prouder of the work
> Than customary bounty can enforce you. (TLN 1731–5, 3.4.4–9)

The Norton Shakespeare glosses just one word in this speech – 'lover' – and does so with the word 'friend'. Masten generously observes that the edition

Shakespeare: Critical Reference Edition (Oxford University Press, 2017), pp. 2: 1519–1520.

in question is 'arguably the most feminist and the least homophobic complete-works edition of Shakespeare ever produced', but he notes that 'there are still moments ... where queer possibilities are actively foreclosed'. 'Friend', he agrees, is 'accurate' enough but, given the nuances of the rhetoric of same-sex friendship in early modern England, it is not sufficient. The modern word 'friend', he notes, 'must be regarded in many ways as a false cognate of the early modern term'.[77] Rehearsing the rhetoric of Antonio and Bassanio's friendship earlier in the play – Antonio's statement 'My purse, my person, my extremest means / Lie all unlocked to your occasions' (TLN 146–48, 1.1.138–9), for instance – and observing that Lorenzo's description of Antonio as Bassanio's 'lover' 'occurs at a moment in which Bassanio's relation to Antonio begins most strongly to be in tension with his relation to Portia, and [at] the beginning of her own expanded power in the play', the gloss, Masten suggests, serves to leave 'the *philos* standing while deleting *eros*, the possibility of eroticism or sexual acts between men, especially if these are regarded as mutually exclusive of erotic, sexual, or marital union with women'. Masten concludes by suggesting that the gloss functions, in effect, 'as an editorial emendation'.[78]

This, obviously, is a great deal of pressure to put on a single gloss. For Masten, it would seem, such a gloss – a one-word gloss of a single word in the text – can never be adequate; a commentary note, at the very least, probably one connected to a discussion in the introduction of the play's dramatization of same-sex relations would be required. This arguably doesn't help the editor who has been tasked by the publisher with providing glosses and not CNs, but it does draw attention to the ramifications of choosing to create such a gloss. Why might an editor choose, at this moment in *Merchant*, to gloss 'lover' as 'friend'? Masten finishes by asking his reader to 'think about how glosses in our editions of Shakespeare can blind us to other, more complex histories of sexuality, gender, and race in these plays and the culture in which they were produced'.[79] Queer theory, in other words, can make an important difference to editorial practice.

---

[77] Jeffrey Masten, *Queer Philologies: Sex, Language, and Affect in Shakespeare's Time* (University of Pennsylvania Press, 2016), pp. 223–226.

[78] Masten, *Queer Philologies*, p. 226. [79] Masten, *Queer Philologies*, p. 227.

Our third example of a textual/critical intersection is the most recent, and it addresses another area of 'blindness' in the editing process. We have more than once mentioned the tendency of the New Bibliography to understand early modern textual processes through binaries and in particular through the binary 'fair'/'foul' proposed by W. W. Greg as a means of differentiating the kinds of copy from which a printer printed a play text.[80] Brandi K. Adams reads this binary through the lens of premodern critical race theory. She notes the textual work of Paul Werstine, Tiffany Stern and others in questioning the value of fair/foul as a means of understanding copy but chooses to address it from a different perspective, that of 'the wider structural inequities in the field that undergird' the deployment of the binary.[81] To do this, she develops an analogy, 'Shakespeare is to text as fair is to foul', one designed to provoke rethinking each term involved. Drawing on work by critical race scholars, she notes that 'fair' in early modern discourse, as well as being a marker of whiteness and beauty, also becomes the 'distinguishing asset of the dominant class',[82] one that could be acquired over time by processes of conversion or aspiration (the beautification of an 'upstart crow', for instance). She cites a series of moments in the Shakespeare canon in which fairness and paper are closely associated – Lorenzo, for instance, recognizing Jessica's letter, says: 'I know the hand: in faith, 'tis a fair hand; / And whiter than the paper it writ on / Is the fair hand that writ' (TLN 805–807). She then turns to Heminges and Condell's claim in the First Folio that Shakespeare wrote so flowingly that they 'scarce received from him a blot in his papers' and the implication of this claim that the fairness of Shakespeare's Folio text is to be set against the distinctly

---

[80] W. W. Greg, *The Editorial Problem in Shakespeare* (Oxford University Press, 1954).

[81] B. K. Adams, 'Fair/Foul', in *Shakespeare/Text*, ed. Claire M. L. Bourne (Bloomsbury Publishing, 2021), pp. 24–49 (30). See also Paul Werstine, *Early Modern Playhouse Manuscripts and the Editing of Shakespeare* (Cambridge University Press, 2013); and Tiffany Stern, *Documents of Performance in Early Modern England* (Cambridge University Press, 2009).

[82] Adams, *Fair/Foul*, 34, citing Margreta De Grazia, 'The Scandal of Shakespeare's Sonnets', *Shakespeare Survey* 46 (1993): 35–50 (45).

imperfect mediation of the earlier quartos.[83] Adams notes that this attitude to the nature of the text became the driving principle of the New Bibliography, arguing that 'the perception of Shakespeare as fair and perfect, were it not for the vagaries of textual transmission, became intrinsic not only to his very existence at the centre of the Western canon but also to the editors who elected themselves as guardians of his legacy'.[84] She concludes by citing the work of Evelyn May Albright, an early twentieth-century scholar who, by detailing the multiple processes through which a theatrical manuscript became a printed book and by quietly rejecting the New Bibliographical assumption that publishers worked against, not in collaboration with, acting companies, undermined the assumption of a clearcut distinction between fair and foul copy. In so doing – in, as Adams puts it, 'her ability to work with the deep-rooted messiness involved in the publication of all play quartos and drama folios' – Albright foreshadowed an important strand in current textual scholarship.[85] Her work, however, Adams notes, was sidelined by the men who at that time controlled the field.

Adams thus shows that 'fair' and 'foul', as a mechanism of inclusion and exclusion, can no longer be seen as *either* a modern *textual* binary created by New Bibliographers for different kinds of manuscript copy *or* an early modern *cultural* binary that functioned to include and exclude subjects through racial (or proto-racial) imaginings. Rather, the association of Shakespeare with the 'fair' in textual scholarship is symptomatic of the way in which he – born a white man in England – was not simply 'fair' from birth but *became* 'fair', with all 'the structural, social and political power that accompanies' fairness, in the history of the reception of his writings.[86] In the process, Adams makes it clear that theories that might appear mutually exclusive – of the text on the one hand, of premodern race on the other – are in fact closely intertwined and that their intersection can make visible

---

[83] M. M. Mahood, ed.; Tom Lockwood, rev., *The Merchant of Venice*, The New Cambridge Shakespeare (Cambridge University Press, 2018), 2.4.12–14.

[84] Adams, 'Fair/Foul', p. 39.   [85] Adams, 'Fair/Foul', p. 41.

[86] Adams, 'Fair/Foul', p. 44.

certain exclusions, bibliographical, cultural and structural, that have distorted our understanding of the nature and value of the Shakespearean text.

***

We repeat: who you are as a critic is who you are as an editor. You will bring your critical consciousness to bear on the play text you are editing, and you will (we hope) find new ways of thinking both about your play and about the questions raised by your play, both textual and critical. These examples suggest just three ways in which critical methodologies as they emerge can intersect with, inform and tangibly affect the business of editing. There have been, and there will be, we trust, many more such intersections – and the more scholars who match their critical awareness with bibliographical knowledge, the more there will be.

At the same time, it is necessary to accept that any edition is unavoidably a product of its time. At all stages of editing you must realize that, just as an edition of 1840 dates, so will the one you publish in 2040, and the editor's critical orientation, current as it is when she creates her edition, will inevitably also lose some or all of that currency. Have the humility to accept that you are editing for now – for your own now. Most editions tend, as we have noted, to look dated after twenty or thirty years – that is why re-editing Shakespeare and other early modern dramatists is a necessary intervention over time – but you will find as you edit that you can still learn a great deal from editions created in earlier centuries. Most editors of Shakespeare, for instance, develop a particular fondness for certain pioneers in the field. For GM, editing *Henry VIII*, this was the eighteenth-century editor Edward Capell, whose work was largely disparaged by his contemporaries but who was in many ways ahead of the game, at least from a twenty-first-century perspective. For SG, it was Edmond Malone, who made brilliant emendations to the incoherent quarto of *Pericles*. But no matter the achievement of a given edition, it will date.

Stanley Wells wisely wrote: 'I accept . . . that my own editorial work will dwindle into obsolescence, forming one thin layer in the coral reef of editorial effort, like that of my predecessors'.[87] He was right, unavoidably

---

[87] Wells, *Re-Editing*, p. 3.

so, and right, too, to note that the work of editing is cumulative. A coral reef, as we all know, is a vastly diverse ecosystem crucial to the health of oceans that takes a very, very long time to build. And it is a thing of profound beauty. Editing may not have quite the depth and wonder of a coral reef, but it is not so bad, we believe, to have a role, even if fleeting, as an agent in the growth and development of such an endlessly fascinating field of scholarly endeavour.[88]

---

[88] For a Further Reading list, please see the pp. 93–100.

Further Reading

Adams, B. K., 'Fair/Foul', in *Shakespeare/Text*, ed. Claire M. L. Bourne (Bloomsbury Arden Shakespeare, 2021), pp. 29–49

Adams, Brandi, 'Editing Shakespeare and Race', in *The Oxford Handbook of Shakespeare and Race*, ed. Patricia Akhimie (Oxford University Press, 2024), pp. 529–545

Bentley, G. E., *The Jacobean and Caroline Stage*, 7 vols (Clarendon Press, 1941–56)

Blake, N. F., *A Grammar of Shakespeare's Language* (Red Globe Press, 2002)

Bland, Mark, *A Guide to Early Printed Books and Manuscripts* (Wiley-Blackwell, 2010)

Blayney, Peter W. M., *The Texts of King Lear and Their Origins*, vol. 1: *Nicholas Okes and the First Quarto* (Cambridge University Press, 1982)

Bourne, Claire M. L., ed., *Shakespeare/Text: Contemporary Readings in Textual Studies, Editing and Performance*, 'Arden Shakespeare Intersections' (Bloomsbury Arden Shakespeare, 2021)

Chambers, E. K., *The Elizabethan Stage*, 4 vols (Clarendon Press, 1923)

Dawson, Giles E., and Laetitia Kennedy-Skipton, *Elizabethan Handwriting 1500–1650* (W. W. Norton, 1966)

De Grazia, Margreta, 'The Scandal of Shakespeare's Sonnets', *Shakespeare Survey* 46 (1993), pp. 35–50

De Grazia, Margreta, and Peter Stallybrass, 'The Materiality of Shakespeare's Text', *Shakespeare Quarterly* 44.3 (1999): 255–283

Dent, R. W., *Shakespeare's Proverbial Language: An Index* (University of California Press, 1981)

Dent, R. W., *Proverbial Language in English Drama Exclusive of Shakespeare: An Index* (University of California Press, 1984)

Dessen, Alan C., and Leslie Thomson, *A Dictionary of Stage Directions in English Drama, 1580–1642* (Cambridge University Press, 1999)

Dutton, Richard, *Shakespeare, Court Dramatist* (Oxford University Press, 2016)

Egan, Gabriel, *The Struggle for Shakespeare's Text: Twentieth-Century Editorial Theory and Practice* (Cambridge University Press, 2010)

Erne, Lukas, ed., *The Arden Research Handbook of Shakespeare and Textual Studies* (Bloomsbury Arden Shakespeare, 2021)

Erne, Lukas, *Shakespeare and the Book Trade* (Cambridge University Press, 2013)

Erne, Lukas, *Shakespeare as Literary Dramatist* (Cambridge University Press, 2003)

Erne, Lukas, and Margaret Jane Kidnie, eds, *Textual Performances: The Modern Reproduction of Shakespeare's Drama* (Cambridge University Press, 2004)

Foucault, Michel, 'What Is an Author' (1969), in *The Book History Reader*, eds. David Finkelstein, and Alistair McCleery, 2nd ed. (Routledge, 2006), pp. 281–291

Gaskell, Philip, *A New Introduction to Bibliography* (Oxford University Press, 1972)

Gossett, Suzanne, *Shakespeare and Textual Theory* (Bloomsbury Arden Shakespeare, 2022)

Greetham, D. C., *Textual Scholarship: An Introduction* (Clarendon Press, 1999; first published 1994)

Greg, W. W., *The Editorial Problem in Shakespeare* (Oxford University Press, 1954)

Greg, W. W., 'The Rationale of Copy-Text', *Studies in Bibliography* 3 (1950–51): 19–36

Hinman, Charlton, *The Printing and Proof-Reading of the First Folio of Shakespeare* (Oxford University Press, 1963)

Honigmann, E. A. J., *The Stability of Shakespeare's Text* (Arnold, 1965)

Hope, Jonathan, *Shakespeare's Grammar* (Bloomsbury Arden Shakespeare, 2003)

Jowett, John, 'Shakespeare and the Kingdom of Error', in *The New Oxford Shakespeare Critical Reference Edition*, ed. Gary Taylor and others (Oxford University Press, 2017), vol. 1, pp. xliv–lxiii

Jowett, John, *Shakespeare and Text* (Oxford University Press, 2007)

Kidnie, Margaret Jane, 'Text, Performance, and the Editors: Staging Shakespeare's Drama', *Shakespeare Quarterly* 51 (2000): 456–473

Kidnie, Margaret Jane, and Sonia Massai, eds, *Shakespeare and Textual Studies* (Cambridge University Press, 2015)

Leech, Clifford, 'On Editing One's First Play', *Studies in Bibliography* 23 (1970): 61–70

Lesser, Zachary, *Hamlet after Q1: An Uncanny History of the Shakespearean Text* (University of Pennsylvania Press, 2015)

Loffman, Clare, and Harriet Philips, eds, *A Handbook of Early Modern Texts: Material Readings in Early Modern Culture* (Routledge, 2020)

Long, William, '"Precious Few": English Manuscript Playbooks', in *A Companion to Shakespeare*, ed. David Scott Kastan (Wiley, 1999), pp. 414–433.

MacKenzie, D. F., 'History of the Book', in *The Book Encompassed*, ed. Peter Davison (Cambridge University Press, 1982), pp. 290–301

MacKenzie, D. F., *Bibliography and the Sociology of Texts* (Cambridge University Press, 2004; first published by the British Library, 1985)

Maguire, Laurie E., 'The Craft of Printing (1600)', in *A Companion to Shakespeare*, ed. David Scott Kastan (Wiley-Blackwell, 1999), pp. 434–449

Marcus, Leah S., *How Shakespeare Became Colonial: Editorial Tradition and the British Empire* (Routledge, 2017)

Marcus, Leah S., *Unediting the Renaissance: Shakespeare, Marlowe, Milton* (Routledge, 1996)

Massai, Sonia, *Shakespeare and the Rise of the Editor* (Cambridge University Press, 2007)

Massai, Sonia, and Andrea Peghinelli, 'Textual Editing and Diversity: *Richard III* as a Case Study', *Memoria di Shakespeare* 9 (2022): 55–73

Masten, Jeffrey, *Queer Philologies: Sex, Language, and Affect in Shakespeare's Time* (University of Pennsylvania Press, 2016)

McGann, Jerome, *The Beauty of Inflections: Literary Investigations in Historical Method and Theory* (Oxford University Press, 1988)

McGann, Jerome J., *Textual Criticism and Literary Interpretation* (University of Chicago Press, 1985)

McKerrow, Ronald B., *An Introduction to Bibliography for Literary Students* (Clarendon, 1927)

McMullan, Gordon, and Suzanne Gossett, 'General Textual Introduction', in *The Norton Shakespeare, Third edition*, gen. ed. Stephen Greenblatt (W. W. Norton, 2015), pp. 75–92

Moxon, Joseph, *Mechanick Exercises or The Doctrine of Handy-works* (London, 1677)

Murphy, Andrew, ed., *A Concise Companion to Shakespeare and the Text* (Blackwell, 2007)

Orgel, Stephen, 'What Is a Text?', *Research Opportunities in Renaissance Drama* 24 (1981): 3–6; reprinted in *The Authentic Shakespeare, and Other Problems of the Early Modern Stage* (Routledge, 2002), pp. 1–5

Preston, Jean F., and Laetitia Yaendle, *English Handwriting 1400–1650: An Introductory Manual* (Pegasus Press, 1999)

Rivzi, Pervez, 'The Use of Spellings for Compositor Attribution in the First Folio', *Papers of the Bibliographical Society of America*, 110 (2016): 1–53

Roberts, Jeanne Addison, '"Wife" or "Wise" – *The Tempest*, l. 1786', *Studies in Bibliography* 31 (1978): 203–208

Rory Loughnane, and Willy Maley, *Editing Archipelagic Shakespeare*, Cambridge Elements: Shakespeare and Text (Cambridge University Press, 2024)

Shaheen, Naseeb, *Biblical References in Shakespeare's Plays* (University of Delaware Press, 1999)

Shillingsburg, Peter, *Scholarly Editing in the Computer Age*, 3rd ed. (University of Michigan Press, 1996)

Stern, Tiffany, *Documents of Performance in Early Modern England* (Cambridge University Press, 2009)

Stern, Tiffany, *Making Shakespeare: From Stage to Page*, Accents on Shakespeare (Routledge, 2004)

Tanselle, G. Thomas, *A Rationale of Textual Criticism* (University of Pennsylvania Press, 1989)

Tilley, Morris Palmer, *A Dictionary of the Proverbs in England in the Sixteenth and Seventeenth Centuries* (University of Michigan Press, 1951)

Wells, Stanley, *Re-Editing Shakespeare for the Modern Reader* (Clarendon Press, 1984)

Werner, Sarah, *Studying Early Printed Books, 1450–1800: A Practical Guide* (Wiley, 2019)

Werstine, Paul, *Early Modern Playhouse Manuscripts and the Editing of Shakespeare* (Cambridge University Press, 2013)

Wiggins, Martin, in Association with Catherine Richardson, eds., *British Drama, 1533–1642: A Catalogue*, 9 vols to date (Oxford University Press, 2012-present)

Williams, Gordon, *A Dictionary of Sexual Language and Imagery in Shakespeare and Stuart Literature* (Athlone Press, 1994)

Williams, William Proctor, and Craig S. Abbott, *An Introduction to Bibliographical and Textual Studies*, 4th ed. (Modern Language Association of America, 2009)

Yarn, Molly, *Shakespeare's 'Lady Editors': A New History of the Shakespearean Text* (Cambridge University Press, 2022)

Shakespeare Editions Cited

All's Well That Ends Well, ed. Suzanne Gossett and Helen Wilcox (Bloomsbury Arden Shakespeare, 2019)

Cymbeline, ed. Martin Butler, 'The New Cambridge Shakespeare' (Cambridge University Press, 2005)

Hamlet, ed. Philip Edwards, rev. Heather Hirschfeld, 'The New Cambridge Shakespeare' (Cambridge University Press, 2019)

Henry V, ed. Gary Taylor (Oxford University Press, 1982)

Henry V, ed. Andrew Gurr, Updated Edition, 'The New Cambridge Shakespeare' (Cambridge University Press, 2005)

Henry VIII, ed. Gordon McMullan (Bloomsbury Arden Shakespeare, 2000)

King Lear, ed. R. A. Foakes, 'The Arden Shakespeare' (Bloomsbury Arden Shakespeare, 1997)

Macbeth, ed. A. R. Braunmuller, 'The New Cambridge Shakespeare' (Cambridge University Press, 1997)

Othello, ed. Norman Sanders, rev. Christina Luckyi, 'The New Cambridge Shakespeare' (Cambridge University Press, 2018)

Pericles, ed. Suzanne Gossett (Bloomsbury Arden Shakespeare, 2004)

Richard II, ed. Andrew Gurr, Updated ed., 'The New Cambridge Shakespeare' (Cambridge University Press, 2003)

Richard III, ed. John Jowett, 'The Oxford Shakespeare' (Oxford University Press, 2000)

The First Quarto of Othello, ed. Scott McMillin, 'The New Cambridge Shakespeare: The Early Quartos' (Cambridge University Press, 2001)

The Merchant of Venice, ed. M. M. Mahood, rev. Tom Lockwood, 'The New Cambridge Shakespeare' (Cambridge University Press, 2018)

The New Oxford Shakespeare: The Complete Works, eds. Gary Taylor, John Jowett, Terri Bourus, and Gabriel Egan (Oxford University Press, 2016)

The Norton Shakespeare, Third Edition, gen. ed. Stephen Greenblatt (Norton, 2015)

The Oxford Shakespeare: The Complete Works, gen. eds. Stanley Wells and Gary Taylor (Oxford University Press, 1986)

The Tempest, ed. David Lindley, 'The New Cambridge Shakespeare' (Cambridge University Press, 2013)

The Tempest, ed. Rory Loughnane, in *The New Oxford Shakespeare: Critical Reference Edition* (Oxford University Press, 2017)

Other Editions Cited

Anon., *Blame Not Our Author*, ed. Suzanne Gossett (Malone Society Collections XII, 1983)

Anon., *Hierarchomachia or The Anti-Bishop*, ed. Suzanne Gossett (Bucknell University Press, 1982)

Anon., *Jacobean Academic Plays*, Collections XIV, ed. Suzanne Gossett and Thomas L. Berger (Malone Society, 1988)

Beaumont, Francis, and John Fletcher, *Dramatic Works in the Beaumont and Fletcher Canon*, gen. ed. Fredson Bowers, 10 vols (Cambridge University Press, 1966–1996)

Beaumont, Francis, and John Fletcher, *Philaster*, ed. Suzanne Gossett, 'Arden Early Modern Drama' (Bloomsbury Arden Shakespeare, 2009)

Fletcher, John, *The Island Princess*, ed. Clare McManus, 'Arden Early Modern Drama' (Bloomsbury Arden Shakespeare, 2012)

Jonson, Ben, *The Cambridge Edition of the Works of Ben Jonson*, eds. David Bevington, Ian Donaldson and Martin Butler, 7 vols (Cambridge University Press, 2012)

Marston, John, *The Wonder of Women, or Sophonisba*, ed. Suzanne Gossett (Oxford University Press, forthcoming)

Middleton, Thomas, and William Rowley, *The Changeling*, ed. Douglas Bruster, in *Thomas Middleton, the Collected Works*, ed. Gary Taylor and others (Oxford University Press, 2007), pp. 1632–1678

Thomas Middleton, and William Rowley, *The Changeling*, ed. Gordon McMullan (Bloomsbury Arden Shakespeare, forthcoming 2028)

Thomas Middleton: The Collected Works, ed. Gary Taylor and John Lavagnino (Oxford University Press, 2007)

Websites

https://folgerpedia.folger.edu/Practical_Paleography

https://beinecke.library.yale.edu/article/quarantine-reading-learn-read-secretary-hand

http://deep.sas.upenn.edu/

www.earlyprintedbooks.com

https://webarchive.nationalarchives.gov.uk/ukgwa/20230801144244/

https://www.nationalarchives.gov.uk/palaeography/

Acknowledgements

We are grateful to the following:

Claire Bourne and Rory Loughnane, editors of this series, for their patience, support and detailed engagement with our typescript. Claire went a long way above and beyond in securing images for us, and we are indebted to her.

Emily Hockley and her team at Cambridge University Press.

The reviewers for the press who both corrected errors and recognised what we were trying to achieve within the bracing word count of an Element. We have benefited from a good number of their corrections and suggestions.

Margaret Bartley, our friend and collaborator on all things Arden.

The general editors of the Arden Shakespeare Third Series – Richard Proudfoot, Ann Thompson, David Scott Kastan and Henry Woudhuysen – for their unceasing support and encouragement.

Our colleagues on *The Norton Shakespeare*, *3E*, above all Stephen Greenblatt and the volume editors, Jean Howard, Katharine Maus and Walter Cohen, and our wonderful team of individual play editors.

John Jowett, our co-general editor for Arden Early Modern Drama, who drafted the series guidelines that were, inevitably, in our minds, along with those we created for *The Norton Shakespeare*, *3E*, as we wrote this Element.

Anne Sophie Refskou for reading multiple drafts and making invaluable suggestions for improving the experience of the reader who has not (yet) edited.

This Element is for Richard Proudfoot,
incomparable editor and mentor

Cambridge Elements

Shakespeare and Text

Claire M. L. Bourne
The Pennsylvania State University

Claire M. L. Bourne is Associate Professor of English at The Pennsylvania State University. She is author of *Typographies of Performance in Early Modern England* (Oxford University Press 2020) and editor of the collection *Shakespeare / Text* (Bloomsbury 2021). She has published extensively on early modern book design and reading practices in venues such as *PBSA*, *ELR*, *Shakespeare*, and numerous edited collections. She is also co-author (with Jason Scott-Warren) of an article attributing the annotations in the Free Library of Philadelphia's copy of the Shakespeare First Folio to John Milton. She has edited Fletcher and Massinger's *The Sea Voyage* for the *Routledge Anthology of Early Modern Drama* (2020) and is working on an edition of *Henry the Sixth, Part 1* for the Arden Shakespeare, Fourth Series.

Rory Loughnane
University of Kent

Rory Loughnane is Reader in Early Modern Studies and Co-director of the Centre for Medieval and Early Modern Studies at the University of Kent. He is the author or editor of nine books and has published widely on Shakespeare and textual studies. In his role as Associate Editor of the New Oxford Shakespeare, he has edited more than ten of Shakespeare's plays, and co-authored with Gary Taylor a book-length study about the 'Canon and Chronology' of Shakespeare's works. He is a General Editor of the forthcoming

Oxford Marlowe edition, a Series Editor of Studies in Early
Modern Authorship (Routledge), a General Editor of the
CADRE database (cadredb.net), and a General Editor of The
Revels Plays series (Manchester University Press).

ADVISORY BOARD

Patricia Akhimie
The Folger Institute
Terri Bourus
Florida State University
Dennis Britton
*University of British
    Columbia*
Miles P. Grier
*Queen's College,
    City University
    of New York*
Chiaki Hanabusa
Keio University
Sujata Iyengar
University of Georgia
Jason Scott-Warren
University of Cambridge

M. J. Kidnie
University of Western Ontario
Zachary Lesser
University of Pennsylvania
Tara L. Lyons
Illinois State University
Joyce MacDonald
University of Kentucky
Laurie Maguire
*Magdalen College, University
    of Oxford*
David McInnis
University of Melbourne
Iolanda Plescia
Sapienza – University of Rome
Alan Stewart
Columbia University

About the Series

Cambridge Elements in Shakespeare and Text offers a platform for
original scholarship about the creation, circulation, reception,
remaking, use, performance, teaching, and translation of the
Shakespearean text across time and place. The series seeks to publish
research that challenges–and pushes beyond–the conventional
parameters of Shakespeare and textual studies.

Cambridge Elements

Shakespeare and Text

ELEMENTS IN THE SERIES

Shakespeare, Malone and the Problems of Chronology
Tiffany Stern

Theatre History, Attribution Studies, and the Question of Evidence
Holger Schott Syme

Facsimiles and the History of Shakespeare Editing
Paul Salzman

Editing Archipelagic Shakespeare
Rory Loughnane and Willy Maley

Shakespeare Broadcasts and the Question of Value
Beth Sharrock

Shakespeare and Scale: The Archive of Early Printed English
Anupam Basu

Textual Genealogies and Shakespeare's History Plays
Gary Taylor and John Nance

Anne Shakespeare's Epitaph
Katherine West Scheil

Collaboration, Technologies, and the History of Shakespearean Bibliography
Heidi Craig, Laura Estill, Kris L. May and Dorothy Todd

Editing an Early Modern Play: A Practical Guide
Suzanne Gossett and Gordon McMullan

A full series listing is available at: www.cambridge.org/ESTX

For EU product safety concerns, contact us at Calle de José Abascal, 56–1°, 28003 Madrid, Spain or eugpsr@cambridge.org.

www.ingramcontent.com/pod-product-compliance
Lightning Source LLC
LaVergne TN
LVHW011846060526
838200LV00054B/4188